'EVENING ALL is Jack Warner's own account of his forty years in show business. But it is also much more than a mere collection of reminiscences.

This is not simply a record of remarkable thespian achievement, but also an intimate and evocative diary of the times. Both public and private lives are chronicled, together with details of Jack's friendships with a host of distinguished entertainers, such as Maurice Chevalier, Sid Field, Tony Hancock, Frankie Howerd and many others, of whom he writes with affection and rare understanding.

'EVENING ALL

Jack Warner

With best
best wishes
Sincerely
Jack Warner

STAR

A STAR BOOK

published by
the Paperback Division of
W. H. ALLEN & Co. Ltd

A Star Book
Published in 1979
by the Paperback Division of
W. H. Allen & Co. Ltd
A Howard and Wyndham Company
44 Hill Street, London W1X 8LB

First published in Great Britain by
W. H. Allen & Co. Ltd, 1975
under the title *Jack of All Trades*

Printed in Great Britain by
Richard Clay (The Chaucer Press) Ltd
Bungay, Suffolk

ISBN 0 352 30342 5

To my Mother

Contents

Foreword

During the past twenty years many friends suggested that I ought to write my autobiography, but I was not sure that the pattern of my life, when unfolded, could be sufficiently absorbing to hold the readers' attention.

Twelve months ago, I discussed the question with my great friend, Norman Lucas, Chief Crime Reporter of the *Sunday Mirror*. Norman is the author of thirteen books and he has also assisted three people in writing their autobiographies.

I told Norman I couldn't catalogue a series of 'sexploits', nor had I any reason to be outrageously critical of colleagues in my profession. He knows that I'm not a person willing to be a controversialist for the sake of capturing newspaper headlines and it is against my nature to employ gimmicks in order to publicise myself. So, stripped of these aspects, which seem to have become essential ingredients in some best-selling autobiographies, I had to ask what would be left of my story?

Norman's reaction was: 'Jack, if such things appeared in your autobiography your fans and friends would know at once the story was phoney.'

Well, it's the factual story that I have set down in these pages. I have exaggerated and embellished nothing. When I finished, a suitable title posed a problem. I thought of calling the book 'I Was Lucky' because in many ways this is true; fate has been kind to me. I certainly wasn't born with a silver spoon in my mouth but I did have an extremely happy childhood. And I was lucky in marriage and in my career.

I have seen fellow artistes reach the peak of the profession only to be toppled by the innovation of television, ill health or marriages that have crumbled. I have been spared such shattering experiences.

Because of the devotion of Mollie, my wife, I was able to overcome financial problems which weighed heavily on me in my early days—before and shortly after I entered show business. Only a fool would deny that a steady income and security represent two of the major assets in life but I found even greater riches in the warmth of a happy family as a child, in my relationship with my wife, and in the genuine friendships that I made and sustained throughout my life.

The title which appears on the cover relates to my work on the longest-ever television series to run on the BBC. *Dixon of Dock Green* kept me employed for twenty-one years. There are the Dads and Mums—probably now the Grandads and Grandmas—who recall the wartime days of *Garrison Theatre*; the Mums and Dads recall my immediate post-war films, including *The Blue Lamp*, *Albert RN* and *Carve Her Name with Pride*, the radio series *The Huggetts* the films of *The Huggetts* and the first *Dixon of Dock Green* television programmes; and maybe their children know Jack Warner only as George Dixon. In all I made over thirty movies.

It just could be that there are also those who remember me in far-off days when I sold motor cars and raced at Brooklands and others who even recall my first show business appearances in the 'thirties with Jeff Darnell in West End night spots long before George Dixon was 'born'!

Perhaps to some readers the many sides of my life will come as a surprise. My entry into show business began in a semi-professional way in cabaret.

Since the *Dixon of Dock Green* series ended I have reverted to one-man shows which I have given in clubs and other entertainment places throughout the country. Now I have started broadcasting again on Radio 4 with what I think I would describe as a composite programme embracing something of my war-time days with *Garrison Theatre*, something of my long career as Dixon of Dock Green and something of my early cabaret days, but all updated to the type of entertainment listeners expect during the present era.

CHAPTER I

I Arrive

As ROTUND as Humpty Dumpty, our family doctor was a cheerful, outgoing individual whose appearances invariably calmed the anxieties of his patients. But on a day in November, 1895, he had no comfort to offer my anxious parents as they received him in their bedroom of a house in Rounton Road, which was well within the sound of Bow Bells.

They had hoped desperately for some reassurances, but the doctor was no longer his jovial self as he examined the pale, frail, six-weeks-old baby boy in the cot. As he replaced his stethoscope he looked up and said, 'Poor wee mite, there's nothing that I can do for him. You'd better have him baptised while there is time.'

Well within the hour a local cleric had performed the christening of Horace John Waters, murmured a few words of solace to my parents, and then left on some other errand of mercy. What passed between them I do not know, but what I can say was that my mother, bless her, refused, despite the doctor's forebodings, to give way to defeat. I owe my survival to her alone and whenever I recall the circumstances of her fight for my life, as they were recounted to me when I was old enough to understand, I am reminded that the most dramatic role I ever played occurred, not in the movies or radio or television, but in a crib when I was only half in this world. I have always maintained that a leading actor is only as good as his supporting cast. It is equally so of my survival.

I was too weak to be breast fed, and my mother's immediate problem was to get me to take enough nourishment to give me strength to defeat death. Post-natal care was hardly known in those days but mother was nothing if not resourceful. Her sole equipment was a fountain-pen filler containing a mixture of her milk plus brandy which she used to force between my lips. Horace John Waters, born October 24th, 1895, was to live and take his place in an extremely happy home alongside brother Arthur and sister Elsie.

My dislike of the name of Horace was understood by my mother and father. They called me John, while Arthur, Elsie, Bernard (always known as Bill), Doris and Leslie, who were born later, all called me Jack.

It was my father's concern for my mother's well-being which almost brought about my early demise. Mother had not been outside the house for six weeks following her confinement, but finally he persuaded her to go out to dinner with him. I was left in the charge of my grandmother, but she misjudged the temperature of the bath she gave me. It was far too cold and the shock almost killed me!

Ironically, funerals meant business for my father but he was certainly not keen to boost his income by burying a member of his own family!

Dad, Edward William Waters, was an undertaker's warehouseman—the kind of occupation which, I imagine, would fool panellists on *What's My Line*. He had what he described as a 'natural instinct' for the work which he inherited from his mother who, in her youth, made coffin frillings.

He was first introduced to a pinking room, where the frilling was made, in 1859, where a Mrs Reed and her 'right hand', Miss Elizabeth Parker, operated a workshop in Tottenham

Court Road. Miss Parker and father's mother became close friends but lost sight of each other after my grandmother married.

Years passed, during which time my father was born and attended St.-Giles-in-the-Fields School, Endell Street. Then his family fell on hard times and grandfather, a copper and steel-plate printer, became unemployed during the depression. At the age of nine, my father had to find work to help out and he became a fully-fledged 'doctor's boy' at two shillings and six-pence a week, working from 12.30 to 5 p.m. His job was to carry a square basket containing medicine bottles and it meant he could attend school only in the mornings.

He remained in this long-dead occupation for over two years and during part of the time had yet another job—collecting saws and tools to be sharpened from Maples, Schoolbreds, Hewitsons and the large joinery and pianoforte factories in the neighbourhood of St. Pancras.

When father reached the age of fifteen he heard that a stable boy was wanted by a firm called Messrs. Parker and Abbott in Great Russell Strcet. His mother then learned for the first time that the Parker end of the firm was, in fact, her old friend, Miss Elizabeth, who had started her own business some years previously. She had taken a partner and invested in a pony and trap and when she realised who father really was, he was at once given the job. The business prospered and larger premises were acquired in Rounton Road, but disaster was to follow. Miss Parker's partner became reckless and also neglected the business so that the partnership had to be dissolved. Miss Parker carried on, but with debts of £800—a lot of money in those days.

Competition was keen and, never one to sit around and wait for business to come to her, Miss Parker decided to do her own canvassing for orders and my father became her coachman. This gave him an excellent opportunity of getting to know many undertakers. Dad borrowed money to help to keep the business alive but in 1887 Miss Parker suffered a severe stroke and he was left to carry the whole burden of the concern.

Father borrowed and injected more money into the business for three years until Miss Parker died leaving him the sole executor and legatee with more liabilities than assets, so that he was obliged to go into voluntary liquidation.

Father was pretty desperate and knew that everything would have to be sold to pay creditors. The main tools of his trade were the sewing machines and so that these would not fall into the hands of the Official Receiver he buried them on waste ground.

A year later, father married and re-started the business in what was to become the family home in Rounton Road.

The headquarters of the family and the business would, undoubtedly, have been regarded by any of today's architects as nightmarish and cannot easily be described. From the pavement one saw a two-storeyed building standing among rows of little terraced houses that were a common feature of London's East End prior to World War I.

The ground floor was given over to my father's office and behind it we had a hall, kitchen and dining room. My parents' bedroom—one of six in the house—was on the first floor and I shared another large bedroom with my three brothers.

Alongside the house a pair of large oak double gates opened on to a small cobbled courtyard with stables that housed a wagonette, horses and a little van. Off the courtyard were workshops where coffin frillings and engraved brass coffin plates were produced.

I recall the weird geography of the premises in connection with a farcical event one night during my childhood, when stacks of cardboard boxes in the courtyard caught fire. Three fire engines, each crewed by eight men, were swiftly on the scene.

My father was kindly and hospitable and as the firemen rushed through the kitchen into the yard, he made them pause for a nip of whiskey. Of course, with flames leaping into the air, there was a great deal of confusion.

As an over-awed spectator, I became a little puzzled by the remarkable number of firemen constantly presenting themselves for a swig of Scotch. Curiosity prompted me to count the drinkers and as I reached sixty I realised that the faces were becoming more and more familiar. Six bottles of whiskey later, my father also tumbled to the fact that the men had been running round in circles—in one door, out of another and in and out again.

In those far-off days, my brother Arthur delivered the frillings to undertakers after school and I performed a similar task with the brass plates.

Arthur joined the business and was a well-known figure in the trade until his death twelve years ago. The firm, E. W. Waters (Bow) Ltd., still exists and is now carried on by my brother Leslie and his eldest son, John. I remember how very proud we were of the family business. Our home and premises backed on to the railway. One line belonged to the old North London Railway and the other to the Great Eastern. Then came the great innovation of the District Underground Railway. It caused quite a stir in the neighbourhood, especially as the trains emerged from the underground at Bow Station and ran across a bridge constructed close to the front of our house. This bridge provided father with an advertising outlet because the last thing passengers saw before running into Bow Station was the huge sign, 'E. W. Waters, Undertakers' Warehouseman'. Often, we walked to Bromley-by-Bow Station and then took single tickets to Bow Station just to be able to gaze with pride upon the family advertisement.

Our original premises were demolished by the last but one V2 rocket to fall on London during the last war. By that time, however, the family home had been moved to Prince Albert Road, Regents Park, opposite the zoo. But after the war the Rounton Road premises were re-built.

In the same way that a pathologist is able to carry out a post-mortem with clinical detachment so does an undertaker, or anyone connected with that business, become immune to the drab and dismal circumstances of the daily rounds. We were certainly not a miserable family.

I am quite sure that if our childhood had been shrouded in gloom, my sisters, Elsie and Doris, would have been incapable of creating two such popular vaudeville characters as Gert and Daisy. Every occupation inspires its own brand of humour. I recall that one of the favourite stories among undertakers when I was a young boy allegedly concerned a Cockney spinster anxious to leave all her affairs in excellent order so that, when her time came, her relatives would not be unduly inconvenienced. She visited an East End undertaker to discuss the design of her coffin. When told that it was customary for a single lady's coffin to be lined in white, and that of a married woman in mauve, she was somewhat taken aback. She considered the implications of this and after much thought announced, with some little embarrassment, 'I think that perhaps mine should be lined in white but with just a touch of mauve.' With a bashful half-smile she crossed herself and left.

An East End funeral in those days was an impressive sight whenever some person of prominence in the community was buried, and never more so than when undertaker Archie Adams, a tall, handsome man, was responsible for the obsequies. He had a flair for organising the big occasion, the hearse being drawn along by six black horses plumed with black ostrich feathers and moving with marvellous grace and harmony. Leading the cortège with measured steps, an immaculate figure in frock-coat and top-hat and carrying a polished silver mounted baton, was Archie. He was respected by our elders and even children regarded him with considerable awe.

My brothers and I were keen on roller skating and I remember the day two of us skated to the parish hall to collect a small harmonium which was to be taken to our house. When we reached the place it was obvious that the instrument was much too heavy for us to carry so we decided to place it on our skates and push it home. But we failed to reckon with a steep hill on the way back, and from that moment we could have been justifiably charged with driving a harmonium without due care and attention. It just took off—down the hill—and caught up with the distinguished Archie Adams as he emerged from his business premises. He managed to avoid contact by a whisker but crashed against a wall and then slid with a bump to the ground.

The whole scene could well have been a clip from a Keystone Cops comedy. I expected a good old-fashioned whacking from my father but the Waters' family sense of fun triumphed and the old man booted us out of his office with instructions to apologise to the great Archie while he himself sat down convulsed with laughter.

Father had two horses and Nobby, the pony. I remember Nobby figuring in one of our schoolboy pranks. The age of the family car had not yet dawned but each of us had his own bicycle and we formed quite a cavalcade when mother and father joined us for a spin.

Our annual holidays were always spent at Herne Bay and whenever the occasion demanded, mother would don a bathing costume then in vogue—pantaloons over which she wore some kind of three-quarter-length coat. When we returned home after the holidays, the family bathing costumes were washed and hung outside in the yard to dry. The sight of mother's pantaloons on the line on one occasion proved too much for her young sons to ignore and, unpegging them, we took them into the stable and put them on Nobby's front legs. Closing the stable door we then retired to a safe distance.

Father's reaction hovered between amusement and extreme annoyance, because although Nobby had obligingly lifted his feet so that we could put the passion-killers on him, he resolutely refused to co-operate when father struggled to remove them. Eventually, they had to be cut off and we collected a few sharp cuffs for our pains.

A clip over the ear was, of course, a recognised form of chastisement in those days, and I'm damned sure it did us no harm. The love so freely given to us by our parents forged the strong ties that still exist between the surviving members of the family to this day.

My first real memory of my father was in no way related to his unusual business activities. My earliest recollections of him were as a minstrel—with blacked face, top hat, striped trousers and, of course, a banjo. He loved entertaining with a minstrel troupe and was an accomplished banjo player. My mother had a good voice and it was therefore hardly surprising that they considered music an essential part of our education, and saw to it that each of their six children was taught one instrument or another.

We were all taught to play the piano and I learned to play the violin and later the viola. Arthur was taught the cornet and trumpet; Bill the violin and later the ukelele, when that became a fashionable instrument; Leslie the drums; Doris the tubular bells; and Elsie was also a violinist.

It was fortunate that domestic walls in those days were stout enough to provide some insulation because the cacophony we produced when first we began to play together would have greatly offended the ears of our neighbours.

But although the flats were too often too sharp and the sharps too flat, father decided that if, metaphorically, our bottoms were kicked whenever we struck a wrong note, a certain amount of talent would emerge. We were nevertheless deadly serious about our music-making and delighted when father arranged for a member of the London Palladium Orchestra to visit the house three times a week to lick us into some kind of shape.

We responded to this filip and after a few months the E. W. Waters Bijou Orchestra was born. We couldn't have been too bad because we received a steady flow of engagements for various functions.

Music had always been dad's hobby and in his boyhood he would walk miles just to listen to a band. When he formed our family orchestra, he saw a way in which to raise money for charity.

We had our largest ever audience when we gave a concert for the 1,400 inmates of Poplar Workhouse. Their ages ranged from eight to one hundred years! Our smallest audience was seven—at a meeting of ratepayers held at a mission hall. Our repertoire was more than adequate for a bunch of amateurs. We could perform many different numbers and included hits from current musical comedies.

Father was always thorough in everything and ever on the alert for any sign of talent in any of us. One day, when I was only nine, he heard me singing Harry Lauder's famous song, 'Stop your Tickling, Jock'. A few weeks later, I found myself sitting on my mother's knee in a little hall near Bromley-by-Bow Church in the heart of London's East End, about to be launched upon the great British Public as a solo entertainer!

Father had decided that if I was going to sing Lauder's songs, my 'talents' should be enjoyed by others. But he also insisted that I should be appropriately clad for the part—in a kilt and sporran. To complete my juvenile impersonation of the great Scot, a little crooked stick was deemed necessary. Father scoured Epping Forest until he discovered what he thought was the ideal 'prop'. He peeled off the bark, dried and sandpapered the stick and then gave it two coats of varnish.

When my great moment came, mother eased me off her lap, affectionately patted my rump and whispered, 'Go out there darling, you'll be all right.'

With a million butterflies working overtime in my stomach, I stood before the expectant audience and started to sing. But before I had completed the verse, the perspiration from my hand melted the varnish on the stick, and in turn the stick became wedded to the sporran.

I jumped off the front of the stage in sheer panic and ran all the way home tearful and humiliated. Talk about keeping right on to the end of the road, I felt I had had enough of Lauder and my father's plans for me.

When my parents arrived home hardly a word was spoken. My father appeared crestfallen and gradually I warmed to him because I realised that his embarrassment in front of the audience must have been even greater than mine.

On Sundays mother used to dress brother Bill and myself in

velvet jackets and Tartan kilts. We weren't very mad about this gear because the other East End kids—many of them so poor in those days that they ran the streets bare-footed—were no respecters of others. They were always plaguing us to show them what was beneath our kilts, a question which we considered then to be absolutely outrageous.

Later we were kitted out in Eton suits and Elsie and Doris wore white frocks and had their hair in long plaits. Three of us were in the St. Leonard's Church Choir, Bromley-by-Bow, and during our four or five years as choristers I was for some time the soloist.

I enjoyed this period of my life enormously. The vicar, the Rev. Edmund Sinker, was a marvellous chap. I remember an occasion when I tried to crack a walnut while standing angelically in the choir stalls. It shot from beneath my foot and came to rest beside the vicar as he was about to recite the Litany.

I shall never forget the way the noise of that nut echoed through the silent church. I admitted my guilt when the vicar questioned me later and paid for my sin by cleaning his bicycle. That incident is as vivid today as are my schooldays. I still have friends alive who were fellow pupils at the Coopers Company School in Tredegar Square, Mile End. I was singularly lacking in scholastic ability but I became quite a good swimmer and also had the dubious honour of winning a slow bicycle race two years in succession. For sure, that didn't pave the way to any university!

That was the first time that the bicycle played a part in my life. The second occasion was a little more dramatic. I was riding my cycle to school one day when I skidded in the tramlines and into the path of a big cart-horse pulling a hay cart from Epping to Aldgate. I was saved from serious injury, or perhaps from being crippled, by a policeman who dashed down the steps of Bow Road Police Station and scooped me up in his arms. A little bit of the gratitude to that copper comes out every time I put on my 'Dixon of Dock Green' uniform. I was very lucky!

With school, plus rehearsals and engagements with E. W. Waters Bijou Orchestra, my time was more than fully occupied. We were playing at a certain function when I met a man who later was to exercise a considerable influence on the way in which I presented a solo act to the public—Fred George Weldon.

Fred was a most talented exponent of the one-string fiddle and also put on a marionette show. I was so impressed with his act that I nagged my father until he gave me the marionettes I wanted. He built me a magnificent little stage with beautiful purple velvet drapes—cut-offs from the material used for funeral trappings.

When the drapes were closed they completed my personal motif—a large W with my initials H and J interwoven into it in rich gold.

I really felt that I had arrived in show business. . . .

CHAPTER 2

To the Continent

DESPITE MY appearances as a juvenile before the great British public my actual entry into show business did not take place until many years later. Nevertheless, the performances of the Bijou Orchestra did much to relieve the somewhat drab East End surroundings in which we lived.

Our home environment could not have been warmer or friendlier but some of the streets in the district were crowded with poverty-stricken homes and ill-nourished children. Many parents could only hope that the dawn of a new day might also bring a loaf for the family table.

I have always been a sensitive and somewhat emotional person and the sight of pitifully under-privileged children running around in ragged clothes and often without shoes engendered in me a feeling of guilt.

Superficially, father was strict but he made sure his family lacked nothing and I came to realise that with a trapeze, a three-quarter-sized billiard table and also three good meals a day, we were extraordinarily rich compared to so many other poor souls.

When father died in 1926, I realised that he, too, had been

very conscious of the plight of his fellow men. Among his personal papers we discovered countless IOUs yellowing with age, which revealed that he had helped many needy people over family crises and had never pressed for the repayment of cash willingly 'loaned'. Mother, too, was a very sympathetic person. Constantly she reminded us that we were on earth not merely to help ourselves but to be charitable to those less fortunate in life and I like to think that throughout the years I have never forgotten what she taught me.

The family business prospered, and by 1914 father had moved into a period of change. He disposed of the old treadle sewing machines and replaced them with electric-powered models which enabled him greatly to increase output. He also acquired an old de Dion Bouton car. This really was quite a status symbol and the family put away their bicycles and made ready for trips to places like Epping Forest.

I well recall on our first drive reflecting that life was indeed moving at a pace when I remembered that only a few years earlier father had taken me to the Bow Road at 11 p.m. one night to sit on his shoulder and witness the historic sight of the last horse-drawn mail coach passing on its journey from London to Colchester.

Of course, although only a lad, I just had to have a go at driving Dad's new toy and the air became more than a little blue when I backed it straight into the door to the courtyard!

Father sought to adapt the car for business use and he had a special body built. But the whole scheme was a dismal failure. The body was so heavy that when it was fitted to the old de Dion Bouton the vehicle was hardly able to move.

He then invested in a Model T Ford and used it to deliver trappings to undertakers during the day and for the removal of bodies from hospitals to undertakers during the evenings. Arthur performed the somewhat grisly evening duties for which undertakers paid sixpence a mile.

My introduction to cars sparked off a sudden enthusiasm for motor engineering which, in turn, aroused doubts concerning my future as an entertainer. I became passionately interested in cars of every type and decided to discuss my ambitions with father.

He was an extremely practical and understanding man. If he was at all disappointed at my decision to forsake my early training as a musician and 'artiste' he carefully concealed his feelings. Just as years earlier he had committed us to coaching by a member of the London Palladium Orchestra to improve our abilities as musicians, so he decided on the spot that I should begin a four-year course in automobile engineering at the Northampton Institute attached to London University. I little realised as I passed through the institute's doors in Clerkenwell on a sombre autumn day in 1911 that I was embarking upon one of the most dismal years of my life. I had just celebrated my sixteenth birthday and was agog with anticipation at the thought of taking the first steps towards a career that I was confident was really made for me.

My state of euphoria did not survive my initial year of study and I became depressed and disappointed. I had been stuffed with a bewildering diet of algebra and chemistry, plus other subjects which a diligent student might some time in the future have found useful, but which to me were utterly remote from the greasy cogs that swung into action when a motor-car engine was set in motion.

After my report had dropped through the letter box, I received the inevitable summons to father's study.

When I stood before him, I was relieved to see that he was more perplexed than irate but his greeting was perfunctory. 'What's all this?' he asked, waving the report.

According him the respect one showed to one's father in those days, I said: 'What do you mean, sir?'

'Well, this report is not very good, is it?'

I took a brief look at the miserable record and had to agree.

'Well, what have you got to say about it?'

I decided that it would be better for me to be frank about the situation. 'If you want to know the truth, sir,' I said to my father, 'I think you are wasting your money and I am wasting my time at the institute because I am not learning anything about motor cars.'

Father looked at me for a brief moment and then said, 'Right!' I had learned over the years that when he confined his comments to that one word, he had come to a decision.

Within twenty-four hours, he again summoned me to his study and told me that he had talked to an undertaker who had a cousin in the motor trade.

'The man's name is Mr. Berwick,' said father, 'and I shall take you to see him tomorrow.' Mr. F. W. Berwick was to figure prominently in my life for a number of years.

We drove to Mr. Berwick's garage in Balham. I loved the smell of the grease, the sound of automobile engines exploding into life and I liked Mr. Berwick as soon as I was introduced to him. The following Monday morning I started work—sweeping the garage floor at twopence an hour.

Within a few days I was being taught how to strip down various parts of a car and repair and re-assemble units like clutches and gearboxes. I worked very hard, learned very fast and retired to bed each night exhausted but contented.

At the age of sixteen, I was working alongside a fitter named Charlie Ward, but was much too young to recognise his potentialities. Other people did, however, especially those rich enough to possess a Rolls-Royce. Charlie was able to shed his grimy overalls early in his life and exchange them for Savile Row creations as managing director and then chairman of Park Ward Limited, the world-famous firm of coach builders.

Charlie had a pathological hatred of hearses and in London at that time motorised ones were rare. One undertaker, anxious to acquire a powered hearse, located an old Daimler chassis that he thought could be adapted to the purpose. It was, however, too wide and too short but our foreman, Sidney Thomas, was confident that the problem could be overcome by cutting the chassis in half and riveting an extra two feet of steel inside the frame.

Charlie and I were working on another car one night when the Daimler we had successfully adapted some weeks earlier was brought in for servicing and minor adjustments. It was parked in a corner of the garage and I could see that its presence disturbed Charlie who gave it many a baleful glance until he could no longer contain himself and yelled, 'The bloody thing. Why the hell did they bring it here?'

Charlie had hardly uttered his protest when suddenly and eerily the Daimler engine spluttered into life. 'Cor blimey!' shouted Charlie and vanished hot-foot from the garage.

As a teenager, the possibility of supernatural intervention never occurred to me but I was certainly interested in finding out how a car could start up on its own. I went over to the Daimler which I knew was fitted with a tumbler switch and battery connected to the engine. When I examined the vehicle, I discovered that one of the faults that needed to be rectified was the switch. It had become loose and had dropped, thus starting the engine. It was some time before I could persuade Charlie that no cadaver's ghost had placed a cold hand on the starter.

I realise, of course, that progress over the past sixty years has led to essential changes in industry such as the streamlined methods of mass production, but I often feel that during this vast transition much has been lost in the field of human relations. It was not unusual during my days as a dog's-body to see the guv'nor rolling up his sleeves and donning a grease monkey's garb to cope with some crisis. I remember an incident that occurred after Alex Keiller, the marmalade king, had invested some cash in Fred Berwick's motor business and given Berwick the contract to service his cars, vans and lorries.

One of the lorries, loaded to the gunwales with jars of marmalade—even in those days quite a valuable consignment—broke down near Brighton and we, at Balham, received an emergency call to tow it to London. One of the mechanics, Charlie Heslop, and I, set off for Brighton on a Lacre chassis powered by an old two-cylinder engine. It was tough and strong for a towing job, but a lump had been torn out of the rear nearside tyre, and throughout the drive Charlie Heslop had to keep his arm around me most of the time to prevent me from falling off the open chassis when we hit bumps. We hitched the broken-down lorry to the Lacre and began the return journey, but when we reached Handcross Hill we found it so steep that the only way we could negotiate it was to go up in reverse. And who helped us with our towing problems that night? No less a personage than Alex Keiller, the marmalade king, and Fred Berwick, both of whom had followed in another car to give assistance if required! I can't imagine any big business executive doing that nowadays.

A few nights later, father called me to his study and astonished me by asking, 'How would you like to go and work in Paris?' To say that I was amazed by the question would be an outsized understatement—a Cockney in the East End who had never been farther than Herne Bay and Brighton leaving England to work in Paris! It was like taking a trip to the moon!

Dad explained that Mr. Berwick had telephoned to say that he was going to produce a new car in France in collaboration with the French designer, M. Maurice Sizaire, and he wanted a young apprentice to work on the project with Sidney Thomas, the foreman at Balham. My father saw Berwick's proposal as a wonderful opportunity for me to gain some experience of the world and extend my knowledge of the motor industry and, needless to say, my enthusiasm was boundless.

I must confess that I felt not a little apprehensive as I said goodbye to the family and boarded a cross-channel steamer in August, 1913. Father had paid the price of my one-way ticket from London to Paris—eighteen shillings and threepence!

I was greeted by Mr Thomas and I remember thinking how distinctly English he looked with his walrus moustache and bowler hat, but then so did I. My Harris tweed suit smelt so evocatively of my own country and to this day the tang of Harris tweed is still associated in my mind with the aroma of strong coffee and French tobacco which wafted from every café in Paris.

No time was wasted after my arrival and I was at once taken to the factory in Courbevoie, just outside Paris, to be introduced to M. Maurice and his brother Georges—the latter having been in the famous team of the Sizaire-Naudin cars which won the Grand Prix de France in 1906, 1907 and 1908, a formidable record in those days when competition was equally as fierce as it is today.

Maurice Sizaire was a brilliant designer and an extremely kind man with a great sense of humour. Having left a very happy family, I might have been forgiven for feeling homesick but, living as I did, with M. Sizaire, his wife and daughter, I found myself accepted as a son. My inability to speak French had caused me to be a little apprehensive about my new life but once I was installed in the Sizaire home in the Rue des Entrepreneurs, M. Sizaire swiftly announced his idea for overcoming the language difficulty.

One day, he produced two copies of Charles Dickens's *Tale of Two Cities*—one in English for him and the other in French for me. To improve his English and to enable me to learn French, we each read a few lines from our respective copies of the book and made notes of those words we could not understand. By this method we made surprising progress. Although we hardly got beyond the first chapter, as long as I live I shall always think of the opening lines both in English—'It was on the Dover road . . .'—and in French—'C'était la route de Douvre . . .' Within two months, I was speaking the basic language reasonably well and although my vocabulary was strictly limited, I was able to communicate with those who worked in the factory.

I once asked M. Maurice what I should say if someone asked me a question and I wanted to reply, 'I don't mind if I do' or 'Just as you like'. I didn't notice the twinkle in his eye when he trotted out the equivalent French phrase. About three weeks later, when Madame Sizaire gave a party, to which I was invited, she asked me in French if I would like white wine or red. Having no particular preference I replied with the phrase

M. Maurice had taught me. When the guests seated at the table heard my response they exploded with laughter and was my face red! Later I whispered to my host, 'Did I say something wrong?' He laughingly replied: 'No, no, you did it very well, very well indeed.'

I was unconvinced and pressed him further. 'What did I really say when your wife asked if I preferred red or white wine?'

'You said, "I don't care a bugger one way or the other," ' he replied with great amusement.

The joke was certainly at my expense but it appealed to my sense of fun.

Although I was living in the home of the big boss, I took my place alongside the French mechanics wearing clogs and overalls, and accepted with good grace my share of all the menial and mucky jobs that had to be done. To me, the air in the factory, although polluted with exhaust fumes, was as sweet as a sea breeze at Herne Bay, and I had nothing but admiration for the brilliance and diligence of the French mechanics.

Just a month after my arrival, there began to appear in the French newspapers sensational accounts of the disappearance of Rudolph Diesel, one of the most outstanding men in the industry whose ideas were to result in the production of a revolutionary type of engine.

Born in 1858, Diesel, whose ancestors were all artisans, was trained by his father as a mechanic. His remarkable ability won him a scholarship at the Munich Technical Insitute where he broke every academic record and nurtured the germ of an idea that was to lead to the creation of the diesel engine. He had listened one evening to a lecture by Dr. Carl Linde, the pioneer in artificial refrigeration, who talked about the steam engine and stressed that the best then in use wasted ninety per cent of the energy in the coal it used.

In a notebook that has been preserved, young Diesel wrote: 'Mechanical theory teaches us that only a part of the heat in the fuel can now be utilised. . . . Doesn't it follow that the utilisation of steam or any kind of go-between is false in principle? The possibility suggests itself of putting the energy directly to work. But how can this be done?'

At the lecture he examined a small gadget that resembled a pop-gun which was in fact a cigar lighter. The air in the cylinder, heated by the compression of a plunger, ignited a piece of combustible material and this suggested to Diesel a way in which he might put energy directly to work. He married and settled in Paris as Professor Linde's agent for ice machines, but he worked through many nights trying to design the perfect engine, and often his wife would find him in the morning asleep over his desk. The most minute details of his calculations and ideas were committed to paper and at no time did he abandon his drawing boards for a factory floor.

When he reached the age of thirty-five he published *The Theory and Construction of a Rational Heat Motor*, the result of years of study and investigation. Krupp agreed to finance the invention and in August, 1893, Diesel's first motor was ready for a test. That prototype proved almost disastrous. It produced a blast, which confirmed Diesel's theory about releasing the energy, but the room was showered with metal and Diesel narrowly missed death. But he was convinced that he was on the right track.

Four years later his dream came to fruition when a number of the world's most distinguished engineers gathered at Augsburg to witness a demonstration by a 20 horse-power 'diesel-motor' and were astonished by its efficiency. The advantage of the diesel was that it used the cruder and cheaper forms of petroleum.

In the fifteen years following his successful demonstration, Dr. Diesel acquired wealth and fame and lived in a palatial house in Munich. Vast sums of cash flowed in from his plants established in five countries and in 1912 he visited friends in the U.S.A. to discuss promoting the wider use of his invention. Business tycoons were not greatly interested because fuel was cheap there and they saw no necessity for change. A few months after the American trip he decided to visit England with two friends. One of them was Georges Carels, head of the diesel factory at Ghent.

It was 10 p.m. by the ship's bell on September 19th, 1913, when the trio, on their way to attend a meeting of English manufacturers and to confer with Admiralty officials, broke up and headed for their individual staterooms. Diesel was never seen alive again.

The French newspapers were filled with speculations as to what might have happened to him and there were rumours that he had been killed by the Germans to prevent him from giving technical secrets to the British. After his presumed death it was revealed that he had, in fact, discussed suicide with his son, probably because his affairs were in poor shape and he had been compelled to mortgage his property and was facing bankruptcy.

The disappearance of the near genius was a great loss to the motor industry and was keenly felt by experts such as Maurice Sizaire and his brother Georges.

It was Georges who roused my enthusiasm for motor racing. He was an ace driver and a great friend of Georges Boillot, the number one driver for Peugeot. I had always visualised a racing driver as cool and collected enough to avoid the excitement others are prone to display. Georges Sizaire undoubtedly possessed great expertise but he was the Englishman's caricature of a Frenchman—excitable and voluble. He talked so quickly that his speech bubbled like a syphon of soda water. He was anxious to test my driving ability and on many occasions I went out with him and Boillot.

After a time, Maurice asked me how I was getting along with his brother and when I replied, 'Very well. I can now understand what he says,' he retorted, 'Well, I think you are very lucky because that's more than I can do.'

Not long after the Diesel mystery, I decided that it was time for me to assume some measure of independence commensurate with my eighteen years, so on my birthday on October 24th I moved to a small hotel at Grenelle. It was so close to the Eiffel Tower that I could hear the wireless signals crackling day and night, but to my everlasting shame I never visited the tower.

I used to rise at 6 a.m. for work at Courbevoie and seldom returned to my hotel before early evening. It was a long day but my youthful enthusiasm ensured that time passed unnoticed.

During that October we were getting the first Sizaire-Berwick motor cars ready for the London Motor Show. There was the usual polished chassis and a Coupé de Ville by Labourdette of Paris but the demonstration car was merely a chassis with four bucket seats and was driven from Paris to London by Mr. Berwick and M. Georges Sizaire with M. Maurice Sizaire as the passenger. On the journey to London, the Sizaire brothers decided that the gear ratio of the back axle was too high, making the car's performance sluggish.

A telegram was sent to our factory instructing that I should leave for London with another crown wheel and pinion of lower ratio and I was proud to embark upon the mission—especially as it was my first return visit to the family. They gave me a tremendous welcome, as did the mechanics at Balham who I assisted in the job of modifying the vehicle.

The car, which was really twenty years ahead of its time, was virtually a miniature Rolls-Royce. The shape of the radiator was the same as the Rolls and the faces of the representatives of Rolls who had a stand adjoining ours were truly worth seeing. At that time, the shape of the Rolls radiator had not been patented and therefore Berwick and Sizaire were not infringing any rights.

I returned to Paris with the Sizaire brothers and arrangements were made for the car to be put into full production. The first chassis was completed early in 1914 and I was given the job of driving it to London. Little did we know what a fateful year it would prove to be.

I have vivid memories of that journey through heavy rain and fog to Boulogne where I arrived to see the boat departing.

I wore a *parapluie chauffeuse*, a long rubber mackintosh which covered me from my neck to my feet so I remained dry and, in fact, found the drive quite exhilarating. But the final half-mile of the trip was made across the coal-yards of the quay and the accumulation of dust, smut and the yellow mud of the French roads so changed my appearance that when I stepped down from the driving seat I looked like some giant panda. Amidst a great deal of laughter, a group of Frenchmen hosed me down—at my request.

I finally reached London at 2 a.m. to be greeted by my parents, brothers and sisters as if I had just flown the Atlantic for the first time.

I returned to Paris shortly afterward to spend a great many working hours on the bench and became assistant to the chief tester, a man called Lebouc who, like M. Georges Sizaire, had also driven in the Sizaire-Naudin racing team. He was a splendid character, always full of fun, which suited me because I had by then learned enough French to sing the native songs. Some I will admit were a trifle bawdy but they used to amuse the lads in the factory during lunch break. The boys used to call me Auguste, which was a real compliment because Auguste was then a French clown as famous as Coco.

The cars began rolling out of the factory at the rate of one a week, which compared with today's vast output was laughable but quite good for an independent firm sixty years ago.

I had a secondary role as a chassis driver. With two others, we each drove a chassis to Boulogne or Dieppe for shipment to Folkestone or Newhaven. I began to feel that I was making real progress in my career and was convinced that the valuable experience I had gained in France would be of enormous benefit to me when I returned to England to work.

I still retained enough interest in show business to enjoy visits to the cinema, music-hall and the opera, and it was during this period that I first saw Maurice Chevalier who years later I was to impersonate so often. M. Maurice Sizaire had a secretary, Suzanne du Fresne, of whom I became very fond and one day I arranged to take her to see the 'new comedian'. I had been carefully husbanding my financial resources for this great evening—each franc being worth a shilling—so that I could take my new-found girlfriend by taxi and to dinner after the show.

When we left the music hall after the three-hour performance I displayed all the *savoir-faire* I could muster as we began to stroll towards the restaurant I had selected, but suddenly a man in a peaked cap and goatskin coat came towards us demanding to know why I had not paid him for his services. It was the taxi-driver who had taken us to the theatre and I had forgotten not only to pay him but to dismiss him. His waiting time promptly swallowed all the cash I possessed and made dinner a financial impossibility. There was nothing I could do but walk my sweetie back home. She was very understanding and when she threw her arms around my neck and kissed me good night she said simply, 'Never mind, I still think Maurice Chevalier is marvellous.'

Within weeks of that fractured evening, war was upon us and most of my workmates in the factory were called up for military service. Sadly, many never returned.

On the day war was declared, we had three chassis to ferry to Dieppe, but when we arrived there we were permitted to leave only two of them and had to return to Paris aboard the third.

On another occasion Mr. Thomas and I drove two chassis which we intended to take to London, but on the journey we were halted at a bridge by sentries and turned back. We decided to make a further attempt to cross the bridge and headed for the bridge at high speed. Before the sentries had realised what was happening we were across. In retrospect I realise how stupidly we acted because the sentries were armed and could have picked us off at will.

Inevitably production at the factory ceased and the remaining chassis were ferried to England to be converted into armoured cars for use by the Royal Naval Air Service and the era of the Sizaire-Berwick car in France was virtually at an end. It had lasted barely two years.

I was attached to the French Army as an interpreter and driver at the time when the Germans were driving towards Paris in 1914. Everyone, however, was convinced that the war would be over by Christmas that year, but it was not to be, and in 1915 it became painfully apparent that a long and bitter struggle was inevitable. I decided to return to London and join the Royal Flying Corps, as a driver. Flying was out until later because when I was medically examined the doctors discovered the secret I was trying to conceal—that I was colour blind.

This peculiar disability has always caused minor problems. Many times I have lost snooker matches because I have not been able to distinguish the colours of the balls. Sometimes people ask me what colours I can actually identify. It is a difficult question to answer. What I do know is that when I stand on green grass wearing a suit of a particular shade of brown, the suit and the grass merge into one.

My younger brother Bill did become a pilot but my aeronautics were confined to the observer's seat during flights with some very rash and daring young men in their flying machines. I well recall a trip over Arras one misty day when we missed a church spire by, I am sure, no more than a couple of feet.

I had been posted to an operational Royal Flying Corps squadron as a driver and had to ferry wireless operators to and from the lines. I think I can claim to be the only driver during hostilities who got his Crossley tender balanced upon the edge of one of the second line trenches, at a place called Monchy-le-Preux, which many old soldiers will remember.

I ended up like that on a night of heavy shelling when I lost my way, and I didn't realise what a highly precarious position I had reached until the whole area was illuminated by flares.

At the time I was a flight-sergeant and engaged on a special mission which entailed going up to the front line at all hours to salvage engines from aeroplanes which had been shot down.

We were always on call and one night I had just got my head down when with two or three other chaps I was summoned to the C.O. for a special briefing. We were shown a map and ordered to the front line just beyond Arras to drag one of our aero-engines back to the lines. It was a hazardous operation in thick fog and, ironically, it was only German flares which actually enabled us to reach the engine we wanted. It was no picnic and we were very relieved when our mission was accomplished.

On another night I had a corporal in my squad who annoyed me by constantly wandering around seemingly unaware that he was likely to get his head blown off at any moment. His behaviour prompted me to shout, 'Why don't you sit down and die nicely?' In the tenseness of the night, some of the lads found humour in my remark and it became a bit of a catch phrase. I didn't mean it to be funny and it was no joke for the corporal because he was killed soon after while I was on leave.

I was lucky enough to be awarded the R.A.F. Meritorious Service Medal for my part in these operations.

During my war service, I had another taste of show business. Fifteen of us formed a concert party which we called 'The Aerolites' and it was while I was with this group that I had my first experience of writing entertainment material. I had no idea that I possessed any writing ability but we all used to muck in and scribble gags we hoped were funny. Nevertheless, I discovered that some of my humour seemed to be acceptable to the lads, who wandered into our shows utterly exhausted and with their nerves in shreds after too many weeks in the lines.

When the war ended, I was retained in the Army of Occupation for some time and on Christmas Eve, 1918, I arrived at my civvy billet in a snowstorm and wearing one of the first of the new R.A.F. uniforms. My temporary home was a small terraced house and I walked from the pavement straight into the living room to find eight people seated at a table with curious black marks on their faces. I learned later that they were playing a card game called Black Peter which involved the players having to put soot from the fireplace on their faces every time they lost a trick. After losing five tricks, this meant that a player had a black mark on each cheek, on his nose, forehead and chin. I never did get to understand what the game was really about and I have never again seen it played or even heard of it.

Men in our squadron were going down like skittles every day with Spanish influenza, a killer in the services and also among the civilian population at home. In one day alone fifteen of our chaps died.

I caught it and was delirious for several days. I lived a kind of nightmare when all my wartime experiences floated around in my mind in a series of crazy pictures and patterns that made no sense. I was devotedly nursed by the German woman in charge of the billet and I believe that she saved my life.

Eventually I arrived home on March 31st, 1919, and was given a wonderful welcome by the family. I must confess that my own bed, mother's home cooking and the freedom to take a bath whenever I wished gave me the feeling that I was living in a five-star luxury hotel.

As is well known, work was scarce during those immediate post-war years and to give me a chance to adjust myself to the tempo of civilian life, father suggested that I should help him in the business. I began driving landaulettes at funerals and although burials are sombre and sad occasions humour was not absent entirely from the daily routine. On one occasion a bearer who was sitting beside me as I drove slowly behind the hearse said in what I thought was rather a sanctimonious whisper, 'Don't take any notice of my hat. Somebody nicked mine yesterday and I had to use this old one which is in two parts. I put the rim on first and the crown afterwards and it seems to look all right.' It looked all right inside the car but when he began the slow march with one corner of the coffin on his shoulder, the wind promptly took the top of his hat off! In those days, butchers' meat hooks were used to hang the wreaths on the side of the hearse and we had to be careful that the carriage suffered no damage. In doing so it was not unusual for one of us to find a hook imbedded in our fingers and I knew from experience how painful it could be.

A surprise telephone call from my old boss, Mr. Berwick, terminated my service in father's business. He asked me to work for him again at his factory in Park Royal and I arrived to find the Sizaire brothers already there re-designing the Sizaire-Berwick car. I was not, of course, a green apprentice and they appointed me chief experimental engineer and head tester and I was thrilled—until I saw the modified version of the so-called new Sizaire-Berwick.

Following an arrangement with Rolls-Royce, who now insisted that the design of their radiator should be exclusive to them, the front of the car had been tapered to almost a point. I could accept this structural change but all drawings by Maurice Sizaire now had to be approved by the chairman of the company. Unfortunately he was influenced by an uncle of his who believed he knew everything there was to know about car designing and had insisted that our vehicle was too flimsy and required additional weight and strength. The new car thus came off the assembly line as cumbersome as the Forth Bridge, with a chassis far too solid for the engine. But the chairman's uncle was so confident that he ordered enough materials for a thousand cars. We had made two hundred and fifty of them before the firm went broke and the Official Receiver moved in, but we completed outstanding orders during his investigation. One came from Sir Robert McAlpine, the building contractor, who also asked Mr. Berwick to supply two other cars which were to be used to meet King George V and Queen Mary and their entourage at Cambridge Station, and take them to the new Cambridge Hospital which Their Majesties were to open.

A few days before this event I was testing the car earmarked for the Royal visit and invited my mother to take a ride with me. She was, by some strange coincidence, not unlike Queen

Mary in appearance and was quick to take advantage of the Royal prerogative by reminding me that she had no intention of occupying the back seat without the immediate provision of an extra cushion.

Forty-eight hours before the Cambridge ceremony, Mr. Berwick called me to his office and told me that he wanted me to take charge of the operation and act as driver of the Royal car because, should anything go wrong with it, I would know how to cope with such an emergency. I had to undergo some strange tuition—as a Royal driver!

My do-s and don't-s included never braking the car violently, using the clutch gently, never addressing any member of the Royal entourage unless spoken to and keeping my peaked cap resting upon my shoulder until the party was settled in the car, when I was permitted to wear it.

The programme was completed without a hitch although when Queen Mary got into the car at Cambridge Station, she immediately said, 'I must have a cushion,' and I very nearly forgot myself and replied, 'That's what my mum asked for,' but fortunately the King intervened by asking if the cushion was necessary. The Queen firmly declared that it was.

During the journey I was asked to drive 'a little slower, please', but I was evidently regarded as competent because I was later presented with a gold cigarette case as a memento of the occasion.

The Sizaire-Berwick bankruptcy was not quite the end of the Sizaire saga. In an effort to try and salvage something from the mess, a deal was made in 1923 with the Austin Motor Company and 20 and 12 horse-power Austin chassis were fitted with Sizaire-Berwick radiators and bodies. Because of my esteem for the top-quality Sizaire-Berwick this strange marriage of two totally different vehicles destroyed my pride in an offspring I had seen grow into an aristocrat of the road. It also caused me some embarrassment at the Motor Show when an angry client to whom I had sold a so-called Sizaire-Berwick roundly berated me for deceiving him. He said heatedly, 'You are here under false pretences. I have just visited the Austin stand and looked at their engines and they are exactly the same as the one in the car which you sold me. I didn't want a bloody Austin, I thought I was buying a Sizaire-Berwick.' Cooling him off was no easy task.

M. Maurice Sizaire returned to Paris sadly disappointed and few in the automobile industry thought he would make a come-back, but he did. He designed another car called simply Sizaire Frères which sold very well. I remained on friendly terms with him and regularly visited him until he died a few years ago when I, too, was saddened by the news in a letter from his wife saying: 'Il m'a quitté dans la nuit du 28 Janvier et il repose à Misles-la-Vallée—petite localité au nord de Paris.' He was ninety-two.

CHAPTER 3

The Race Track—and Marriage

THE OLD adage that a door never closes without another one opening exemplified my reunion with show business. When the Official Receiver took charge of the affairs of Sizaire-Berwick in 1921 I became friendly with his clerk, Vernon Lee, who lived in Surrey. Vernon was a keen member of the Sutton Amateur Dramatic Club and one evening he took me along to one of their shows. Some of his enthusiasm rubbed off on me and re-awakened my interests in the stage. It had, I reflected, been my first love. I decided to join the club because it would, at least, add a new dimension to my leisure time. Since my demobilisation I had tended to allow cars and the motor industry to absorb most of my time and energy.

I read for the club and was eventually given the part of Churdles Ash in Eden Philpott's play, *The Farmer's Wife.* I fell in love with the character made famous on the stage by Sir Cedric Hardwicke.

Another play I well remember was *It Pays To Advertise* in which I took the part of an American salesman. I had a very long speech which consisted mainly of advertising slogans such as:

'Beauty your duty.' (Bristow's Soap.)
'Phospherine the greatest of all tonics.'

'Bovril prevents that sinking feeling.'
'More miles on Shell.'
'Your teeth are ivory castles.' (Gibb's Dentifrice.)
'Beecham's Pills, worth a guinea a box.'

There were also references to Pascall's sweets, Wright's Coal Tar Soap, Sandeman's Port, and one stanza which ran:

'If I say His Master's Voice you know it's a gramophone,
If I say Hennessy you know it ain't whisky,
If I say Dewar's you know it ain't brandy,
And you do know that Johnnie Walker does not build bonny babies.'

It is no exaggeration to say that my association with the club was an invaluable experience from which I received my first insight of the rudiments of straight acting. I am a past president of the Sutton club and firmly believe it to be one of the best in the country.

Amateur dramatics were not my only interest and to earn a little extra cash, I took on various engagements at smoking concerts and masonic functions as a comedian. One evening in 1927, when I was taking part in a charity show, I met Nelson Darling, an extremely pleasant chap who was a teacher at Homefield School, Sutton. Nelson was also a pianist, doing a solo act, and we thought it might be fun to team up because he had a ready sense of humour and a personality which blended well with mine. He had no desire to give up his teaching career and at that time I still needed a job in the car business to ensure a steady income. We decided we would be billed as Jack Warner and Jeffrey Darnell. I changed my name to Warner, which was close to my own name of Waters, simply because I didn't want it to appear that I was cashing in on the reputation of my sisters, Elsie and Doris, who were already well known. Nelson Darling's 'new' monniker was a combination job—the Dar of Darling plus the Nel of Nelson and Jeffrey was his other Christian name. He had a good teaching post and was not desperately keen to become known as the master who had switched to show business.

Jeff was an extremely gifted song writer. Today his pseudonym regularly appears when the 'Dixon of Dock Green' titles are rolled on television because he composed the Dixon theme. I discovered that I, too, had the ability to write lyrics, so while he played the piano I did impressions, notably of Maurice Chevalier and Max Miller.

One of my special numbers was to give an impersonation of Max Miller impersonating Maurice singing the number, 'I Was Lucky!' and audiences always appeared to enjoy it. The year 1927 was not only notable for my union with Jeff and the beginning of a friendship which, happily, has continued to this day, but also for my first meeting with Mollie, the girl I was to marry six years later.

She was the secretary to the managing director of Lendrum and Hartman and one evening we wandered off to have a drink together. At the time, she was engaged and I was courting an attractive young girl named Crystal Nye. It didn't occur to me then that had we married it would have been faintly amusing for her to have been addressed as Crystal Waters! We often laughed about it later. She married a doctor and lives in Australia and we still exchange Christmas cards.

To return to my early friendship with Mollie, it was a happy coincidence that one evening after Mollie and I had had our casual drink earlier, I was eating alone in a restaurant in Baker Street when I saw Mollie dining with a girlfriend. Crystal was away at the time and when I chatted with Mollie, she told me that her engagement had ended. Our relationship blossomed and I quickly realised that Mollie was the girl I wanted to marry—when I could afford to indulge in matrimony!

At the time Sizaire-Berwick folded there was a firm next door called Watkins and Doncaster who distributed an Italian car called the Ansaldo. It had been taken over by the sales manager, a Captain Moore, and in 1924 he had asked me to join him.

It was then that I started racing at the Brooklands track at Weybridge, Surrey, which was the rendezvous between the two Great Wars for all budding racing drivers. I owed my enthusiasm for racing to Georges Sizaire, the racing brother of Maurice, who entered the French factory one morning while I was working there. He was waving a French newspaper and was very excited because an English driver, Percy Lambert, had become the first driver to lap the Brooklands track at one hundred miles an hour. He had driven a Talbot. Georges knew the track well as he had tested the Sizaire-Naudin on it. He showered me with congratulations as though I had achieved Lambert's success! Georges' English was not easily recognisable and he repeatedly shouted his praise of the English driver—'Pairsee Lombair'!

My introduction to Brooklands came through a man named Jack Hall, who worked with me at Sizaire-Berwick. Jack was the son of Sir Reginald Hall, head of British counter-intelligence during World War I. Jack sold an Aston Martin to Mabel Lister, a ballet dancer, who asked me to race the car for her. She didn't have to ask twice. I took part in several races over 200 miles and in one of them suffered a back injury that contributed, together with a mishap while filming, to the leg troubles which have so plagued me later in life.

The track was very bumpy in places and at one spot which ran from the bankings to what was called the 'railway straight', cars literally 'took off' and for a fraction of a second were airborne! On one occasion when I hit this patch my cushion shot out of position and I completed the race seated on bare wood. The consequence was that I was cruelly jolted and it did my spine no good at all.

A short steep hill with about a one in three gradient was another feature of the track. At the speed drivers were achieving one had the sensation of driving up the side of a house. A star performer on this hill was Captain Fraser Nash, who drove a car of his own design called a G.N. which later bore his own name. The car he used on this hill climb had a twin-cylinder engine and its performance used to delight the crowds.

Many strange names were given to racing cars between the wars. One of the more notable of them belonged to Count Zborowski and was christened 'Chitty Chitty Bang Bang' and that was a few years before a film was given that title!

It was a formidable looking machine fitted with a Maybach engine and identical with those used by Zeppelin airships. I always thought it a little too powerful for the car's chassis but, to use present-day jargon, 'it really did motor'. The exhaust pipe, which ran to the rear of the car, was about six inches in diameter and nearly five feet from the ground. It was involved in an incident that only witnesses would describe as comic and occurred when the Count took the car to Herne Bay for some speed trials. He was accompanied by a very pretty girlfriend who was extremely interested in racing cars and was always around asking countless questions. On that particular day she was unlucky. She was standing about three feet from the rear of the car with her back in line with the giant exhaust pipe. Count Zborowski hopped into the driving seat and the engine roared. His girlfriend jumped clear but not quickly enough. It was the end of the pretty dress she was wearing and she was never seen again in racing circles!

Another car nicknamed 'Softly, Softly Catchee Monkey' while a French model, a Berliet, which had a reputation for whistling when it reached a high speed, was christened 'Whistling Rufus'. Nobody seemed to know why it whistled but it was an idiosyncrasy that could not be eliminated.

In those days, it was the practice for the driver to carry a mechanic with him in the car. Mine was a lad called Charlie Dando, who is still around today. He was one of the most brilliant engineers I ever encountered during all my years in the motor industry. We worked together throughout the whole of one night, dismantling and re-building a Sizaire-Berwick engine. His brother, the late Fred Dando, was almost equally as skilled as Charlie. He had one strange habit though—he never worked without wearing a bowler hat and inevitably became the victim of a practical joke played by the rest of the team. They inserted a piece of thin copper wire beneath the bowler ribbon and tightened it a little on each of the very rare occasions when Fred took it off. He was utterly baffled and unable to decide whether his hat was getting smaller or his head larger.

I remember one 'crew mechanic' riding with his driver who had completed several laps at Brooklands at about ninety miles an hour when the driver decided that engine adjustments were necessary. He reduced his speed to somewhere between twenty-five and thirty, which seemed much slower to the mechanic than it actually was. He jumped out and promptly turned three somersaults!

It was a pity that the track, which had been the scene of so many memorable events, had to be closed because it was unsuitable for today's powerful single-seaters. At one period I was demonstrating the big 250 horse-power Mercedes-Benz and I often thought that nobody had ever motored until they had driven one of these machines. It had a super-charger that could be cut in at will, and to scream round the banking at Brooklands in this particular monster gave me a sensation that I have never since experienced or forgotten.

The job with Captain Moore brought me further foreign travel. I visited the factory in Italy and the few weeks were most enjoyable. I returned finally to the London showrooms where, of course, I was not only selling Ansaldos but also accepting orders for other makes of cars. I remember selling a Buick through the agents, Lendrum and Hartman, for whom Mollie was then working, to a typical crusty colonel who brought it back time and time again because, he alleged, it was faulty. One day he came in so enraged that he bellowed, 'Waters, if you don't get this car right I'll take it straight back to Fortnum & Masons.' His wrath made him confuse the name of the famous store with the firm of Lendrum and Hartman. On another occasion I was approached by a bookmaker who asked me if I could get him a second-hand Rolls-Royce. I located one and drove it to his house, which was quite small and unostentatious. He tried it out and was most satisfied. Somewhat hesitantly, because a pound was really worth a pound in those days, I told him that the price was £1,500. He made no comment but ambled across the tiny living room to a sideboard, opened a cupboard, removed two vegetable dishes crammed with fivers and tenners and counted out the money. This kind of incident is often repeated today among people like bookies and market stall-holders, many of whom have never been inside a bank let alone had a bank manager in their cupboard!

During this period I was something of a rudderless ship. I could not seem to settle and when an American offered me work as a salesman with his firm, Fada Radio, I went to see him at his office in Kingsway. After being shown the product I accepted the job with some alacrity because I felt that for the first time since working upon the original Sizaire-Berwick in France I would be offering the public something they had never seen before. In the mid-twenties the marketing of a radio which operated without an aerial was almost as revolutionary as the invention of television some years later.

The sets were housed in beautiful wooden cabinets and retailed at £20 each. I took some of them to show the boys in the motor trade and they were extremely impressed, especially when I told them that the dance music to which they were listening was coming from Madrid. It was a terrible gaffe because a moment later a voice announced, 'You are listening to the Savoy Orpheans from London.' But I still sold six sets.

I did not remain in my new job for long—only a year, from 1925–6—because I didn't know enough about the trade to give my sales talk an authentic appeal. People wouldn't listen to me when I told them that one day they would be driving around with radios installed in their cars. I returned to the motor business as service manager at Car Mart Ltd of Park Lane. The firm had a showroom in Euston Road and a service station in Upper Montague Street. I was given one of the best cars of the age to run around in—an Austin Seven—and because of the extent of my experience of automobile engineering, I was well respected by the staff, who often saw me roll up my sleeves and demonstrate how various jobs should be done.

We were Austin agents and I had been with the firm a few months when one of the Birmingham chiefs arrived for a conference with our chairman, Major Grigg, and the managing director, Captain Bowman. Later, I received a telephone call from Park Lane to the effect that the visitor's car, an Austin 20, had broken down and that another car was required to get him to the station so that he could return by train.

I asked what had happened to the Austin and my Park Lane boss said that the director thought the timing chain had slipped. I had dealt with this kind of situation before and when I heard that the visitor had an hour to spare before catching the train I undertook to put the car right before then. My guv'nor didn't believe it could be done, but I hurried over to Park Lane with my foreman, slackened off the timing chain a little, checked the timing through the flywheel cover and put the car in gear. I then got the foreman to jerk the back wheel and we jumped the chain back again. The Austin director watched us and was staggered that his car was ready for the road within ten minutes. A month later, my boss, Major Grigg, gave me a hundred pounds tax free and a rise of six pounds a week. In those days that really was money.

At this particular period my income was quite healthy because Jeff and I were making a few quid several evenings a week at various functions. On June 22nd, 1927, we were both confident that fame was around the corner, having been booked for a broadcast with Jack Payne and the B.B.C. Dance Orchestra from Savoy Hill at 3 p.m.

Although listeners were not going to see us, we presented ourselves at the studio immaculately dressed and well groomed—in those days even the news readers wore evening dress as they stood before the microphone. I had sneaked away from my work at Car Mart and wasn't quite sure how my boss might react if he happened to hear the broadcast. In fact he didn't.

John Sharman, the producer, called us for rehearsal at 2.45 p.m. but he arrived late and then promptly cut our main number because we had used a word in it that was racially offensive. When the red light flashed to let us know we were on the air neither of us quite knew what we were going to do and we played for five minutes instead of eight. We were not well received by the B.B.C. and we didn't get a return date!

We were distinctly gloomy when we left the studios and at that moment, I was quite convinced that I had no future as a professional entertainer.

A few months after this incident, I left Upper Montague Street to become general manager at another off-shoot of Car Mart called Car Mart Garages Ltd., in Balderton Street, opposite Selfridges' main entrance. There were eight pumps on the forecourt, but because the premises were tucked away in a side street, business was not too good and I wondered how the devil I could boost the takings. Then I had an idea. I bought a big stock of small tins of oil and yellow dusters and gave one to each taxi-driver who pulled in for petrol. They spread the word around and business began to look up immediately —in fact it was trebled.

One day a representative of the India Tyre Company called to see me to discuss the merits of his product. He was very convincing and eventually I asked him to let me have two of his tyres, size 820 × 120, to try out on a Hispano Suiza which had such fierce acceleration that the owner of the car found that the life of his rear tyres did not survive 3,000 miles. The India tyres were fitted and easily proved their worth, covering 7,000 miles showing little signs of wear. I then suggested to Major Grigg that we might become India concessionaires in London and the Home Counties. He agreed and we took £30,000 worth of stock. I led a force of eight salesmen and we called upon as many garages as we could and really boosted profits.

When we acquired the Mercedes agency I handled the sales, and then later joined another company selling Alvis, but my feet were becoming very itchy and I felt I had had enough of working for other people.

It was 1933 and I decided to take a gamble and open my own small garage in St John's Wood. Had I known as much about book-keeping as I did about automobile engines I would have realised at the outset that I was too under-capitalised to succeed. My brother Arthur generously loaned me money to try and keep me afloat but I was badly let down by many people who had promised to buy cars from me and failed to do so. However, one man who did keep his word was Sir Ronald Gunter to whom I sold a Hillman.

As an independent dealer at the 1934 Motor Show, I introduced Sir Ronald to the Mercedes-Benz stand. He admired a big two-seater with a gun-metal finish, pig-skin upholstery and left-hand drive and I knew that if I could persuade him to buy the car, Mercedes would happily pay me commission.

After strolling around the car more than once he suddenly halted and said, 'If I buy the car, will you come on the Monte Carlo rally with me?' I agreed on the understanding that we shared the driving and changed over every two hours. Having spent so long in France I was familiar with the Monte Carlo route and knew it was a damned long drive from the north of Scotland to Monte. To his astonishment and mine we completed the rally and won a third prize, but the trip was not without some excitement. At one point we rounded a bend in the mountains not far from the finishing line to find a cart across the road. We were driving at speed and I finally braked to a halt on the very brink of a sheer drop of a thousand feet.

Despite the worries and problems which tended to haunt me during my time as a garage owner, I had another lucky break in my life—I married Mollie at St Mark's Church, Albert Road, Regent's Park. We had been courting for six years so she was well aware of my somewhat chequered career and under no illusions about my parlous financial state.

Mollie carried on working to help me to pay some of my debts and when she had finished her own job, she came to my garage to take care of the book-keeping. The financial picture in those books became more and more depressing. I had never possessed the ability to husband resources but Mollie flogged herself to death to try and keep me afloat.

I didn't need a prophet of doom to tell me which way I was heading.

The few cards I still held in my hand suggested that despite certain disappointments, such as the broadcast failure, I might yet manage to earn a living on the stage. My sisters, Elsie and Doris, were rapidly making a name for themselves. They had followed their plan with unswerving determination. It had been show business from the very beginning and now they were reaping the reward.

One day they were asked to record one of their musical numbers and while waiting in the studio, they filled in their time by rehearsing part of the act they planned to do at a function that evening—an encounter between Gert and Daisy, two Cockney women. They had just finished when the recordist entered the room and asked them what they were doing.

Elsie and Doris gave him a brief run-down on their new act and he told them to go through it again. On hearing the exchanges he was so impressed that he declared, 'We are going to record it now.' Gert and Daisy were thus launched upon the British public. Elsie's violin went under the sofa and the sisters became Gert and Daisy upon theatre bills throughout the country.

There was one occasion when my prowess and experience with racing cars came in very useful to my sisters. They had gone to Folkestone to do a Christmas show, only to discover that they had left their luggage containing their evening dresses behind at their London home. I received a frantic telephone call, snatched up the cases and covered the seventy-five miles from London to Folkestone in ninety minutes, delivering the dresses seconds before they were due on stage.

When they went to France for the first time around 1933 I accompanied them because they were not accustomed to driving on the right-hand side of the road. They tried to persuade me then to chuck the motor trade and have a go at show business and I thought more and more about it on my return when I found that the garage ledger contained figures that signalled disaster.

While in this mood of depression a bloke brought in his car to the garage. It really was in a shocking state but he said, 'If you can get it right so that I can use it tomorrow, I'll buy a new model from you in two days' time.'

Several spare parts were needed to complete the repairs but I just didn't have the cash to buy them so I wandered along to a pub called 'The Volunteer' in Baker Street for a pint and to mull over the problem. It was there that I picked up the racing edition of one of the London papers and saw that Freddy Fox, one of the great jockeys of his time, was riding a horse called Don't Care. The pint—they sold real beer in those days—must have given me a lift because I decided that the name of the nag matched my mood.

I have never been a betting man or known enough about the sport to fancy my chances of picking a winner, but occasionally I have had a flutter. I had only a quid in my pocket and the urge to gamble on Don't Care became stronger as I downed another pint. I left the pub and was about to cross the road when I was forced back on to the pavement to avoid being clouted by an errand boy merrily whistling and riding a box-bicycle bearing the name—F. Fox, Fishmonger. The coincidence was now too great for me to resist a bet. I stepped into a telephone booth, called a bookmaker I knew well and asked him if he would trust me for a fiver on Don't Care. 'Of course I will,' he said, 'but you must be raving mad. I've never heard of the nag, what is it—two men in a skin?'

Maybe it was two men in a skin but it trotted up at twenty to one and with my fiver on the nose I collected £100 later that afternoon—something I'd never done before and have never done since! I managed to buy the spares I needed and worked all night with my foreman to get the customer's car on the road. And he *did* buy a new car two days later!

The balance of my winnings kept me afloat for a short time, but the debts piled up and I was forced to put up the shutters. The year was 1935 and Jack Warner left the motor industry for the last time. . . .

CHAPTER 4

Cabaret and Garrison Theatre

THE WEST END debut of Warner and Darnell didn't bring any rave reviews in the newspapers—in fact it didn't rate a mention anywhere except on my bank account where the red figure was slightly reduced. On the evening of June 24th, 1935, and given only a fortnight to rehearse, we appeared at the Café de la Paix in Swallow Street and Casani's Club in Regent Street, just opposite.

Two main factors prejudiced our success. The first was our meagre repertoire of songs which necessitated the writing and rehearsal of new material in too short a time, and the second was a terrific heat wave which hit London and flattened everybody who could not get out of town for a breath of good clean country air. We opened at 11.30 p.m. at the Café de la Paix and faced our audience—a pair of young lovers who needed us as much as a bride and bridegroom need a mother-in-law on their first night. To add to our discomfort, I noticed a theatrical agent quietly taking a seat at a table with the obvious intention of discovering if we were worthy of his services. Our impact was as great as a floating feather hitting a quilt. We left for Casani's, where we were due to appear thirty minutes after midnight.

Our performance there was practically a repetition of the earlier one, except that a friend of Jeff's, Jack Miller, had rustled up a party of eight to give us some support. Without them the place would have been empty. For the occasion we both wore, regardless of cost, full evening dress complete with red carnations—rubber ones! After the show we hailed a taxi and directed the driver to Canfield House, Finchley Road, where I was then living and I remember turning to Jeff and saying solemnly, 'We're like two bridesmaids returning from a bloody funeral!'

We were booked again for Casani's some weeks later—at a reduced fee, but things did improve when we had mastered new material, and eventually we were to become a great success there. Realising that I now had to depend wholly upon this work for my livelihood, I worried a lot about what our reception would be and not unnaturally, the tension sometimes upset my stomach. One night, as we were awaiting our call in the ante-room at Casani's, Charlie Kunz and his band left the rostrum and the spotlight was turned on for our entrance. Suddenly I gasped to Jeff, 'Hang on, I must go to the lav.'

After what seemed a lifetime to Jeff, Casani ran towards him, flustered and panicky, and in more than a stage whisper growled, 'What the hell's the matter—get on, get on, they're waiting for you out there.' When he heard Jeff's explanation, Casani bellowed, 'Bloody hell, what a bloody fine time to do one.' He shouted to Della, the head waiter, and Tom, the wine steward, to get me out of the loo pronto. I was still struggling into my jacket as we made our entrance.

The public seemed to like what we had to offer and our engagement book gradually filled and we appeared regularly at most of the hotels and night spots in the West End, including Quaglino's, Romano's, the Carlton, Ritz, Piccadilly, Strand Palace, Trocadero, Claridges, Dorchester, Mayfair, New Scala, Savoy, Café Royal, Park Lane, Café Anglais and Chez Henri in Long Acre.

The Piccadilly proved a tough test because when people were eating there they took very little notice of the cabaret. Eventually, Jeff and I became very exasperated with the audience and one night, as we again prepared to battle against the clatter of cutlery and unsubdued conversation, I said to Jeff, 'Take no notice of anything I do tonight. Just continue playing . . .'

The head waiter was a very sympathetic chap so I quietly whispered in his ear. Minutes later, I filled my tails with old knives, forks and spoons.

We began our act and fought hard to be heard above the hubbub. It was then that I stepped on to the dance floor and promptly emptied my pockets. The crash silenced the customers, who paused in their eating and stared at me in amazement. In the silence, I calmly said, 'Thank you very much for your attention. Perhaps you will now listen to the cabaret.' We resumed our act without further interruptions. It was a successful move. The management had booked us for a week but they extended the engagement for another three! It was my first experience of fighting an audience but it wasn't my last. We often had a similar struggle at Romano's, where one of our numbers, 'Sally the Circus Queen', called for me to wear a top hat and to crack a ringmaster's whip.

One night a party of twelve arrived and one fellow with a raucous voice began telling jokes and creating a disturbance among his group. I told him to shut up and when he became belligerent I asked him if he wanted to take me on. That quietened him but he had the good manners to return the following night to apologise for his behaviour and to buy each of us a bottle of champagne.

On another occasion we performed a number called 'The Legionnaires'. It caused an irate and somewhat inebriated lady to complain after the show that we had insulted the French. She was only mollified after we had slowly taken her through every line of the song and satisfied her that none of the words were in any way derogatory.

Another incident, rather more sinister, occurred when John Quaglino was absent one night and I did a burlesque of Adolf Hitler. On that very evening, Herr von Ribbentrop, the German Ambassador to London, and members of his Embassy were dining at the restaurant—without our knowledge. Quaglino received a very strong protest from the German Embassy and we later learned that our names had been placed on Hitler's black list. If the Jerries had successfully invaded Britain our destination, with others, could have been the gas chamber. Fortunately for Jeff, he just escaped capture at Arras in 1940 when he was serving with the British Expeditionary Force!

We did receive a little recognition at this time. The *Daily Mail* on July 9th, 1936, reported, 'Quaglino has been congratulated on all sides for his excellent cabaret turn, Warner and Darnell.'

Nevertheless, we were still extremely nervous when we made our first appearance at Romano's. Initially we had some difficulties and once I bounded up the stairs to the balcony in pursuit of a man who tried to sabotage our act but the twenty-five club hostesses, all beautiful girls, were marvellous, and it was they who persuaded the diners to give a break to the two husky six-footers who were trying to win a duel with the audience.

We cut two records for Parlophone and both had good reviews in 1936, the year we were again auditioned by B.B.C.'s John Sharman. After hearing a number of songs he said that he was not impressed as we had nothing to offer that differed from other double acts. Jeff had just written 'The Legionnaires' and that did the trick. After we had struggled through it Sharman booked us for several radio 'Music Hall' programmes and we always opened the show with this number. The show Jeff and I both remember best was broadcast on March 27th, 1937. It was a request programme and artistes were booked as a result of a *Daily Sketch* variety popularity poll. We shared the bill with five other double acts—my sisters, Elsie and Doris Waters, the Western Brothers, Alexander and Mose, Clapham and Dwyer and Charlie Kunz accompanying Vera Lynn. Unfortunately, despite all the preceding ballyhoo, the programme was not favourably reviewed.

Jeff's number 'The Legionnaires' really did click during those years. We made a short film entitled 'The Legionnaires' which was later shown—on a British Railways express! The film was also taken off the shelf, given a dusting and used by Brian Inglis during the I.T.V. series *All Our Yesterdays*.

Of course, during this period, our late working hours did not unduly affect me because I was a full time professional but Jeff, who was living the Jekyll and Hyde existence of a teacher by day and vaudeville artist at night, was having to stretch himself.

We did a show at the Royal Beach Hotel, Southsea, on May 10th, 1937—the Royal Navy Review Night—and left the hotel at 1.30 a.m. to drive back to Jeff's home in Banstead, Surrey. I was at the wheel and told Jeff to get a couple of hours' sleep. Jeff surfaced at 7 a.m. and found to his astonishment and concern that we were still in Southsea. I, too, had been so exhausted that I had decided to continue driving would have been too risky. For once, Jeff failed to reach the school in time for morning assembly! It became apparent that he could not go on indefinitely leading his double life. London bookings presented no problems, but to travel to provincial towns and then have to rush back in the early hours of the morning in readiness for a day's teaching was just too much.

Finally, in 1937, after we had done a three weeks' season in Aberdeen with Harry Gordon—Jeff only managed to fulfil this booking because it was during the school holidays—he decided that he would have to confine his show business activities to local engagements with his own orchestra.

I cannot pretend that I looked forward to presenting a solo act. Together we had sailed through some troubled waters and overcome many problems and many tough audiences, finally to achieve recognition and win a degree of popularity. I felt that

I would have to face the self-same difficulties all over again and indeed I found it tough as I tried to perfect a one-man show.

A lucky break came for me when Rex Newman invited me to join the famous Fol-de-Rols, a company which was split into various concert parties. I became a member of what we called Rex Newman and his Dancing Coachmen in 1938. We did a week at Torquay as a 'try-out' and then began a three months' summer season at the White Rock, Hastings. I found myself working with Arthur Askey and Dickie Murdoch, who had already established themselves on the radio with their show *Band Waggon*. They worked wonderfully together and introduced to their stage act incredible characters like Nausea Bagwash from the radio show.

Dickie christened me Whimsical Warner and Arthur was dubbed Audacious Arthur. Known to radio fans as Stinker Murdoch, Richard was Dirty Dickie to us.

I have enjoyed a friendship with Arthur for more years than I care to remember and he is, in my opinion, one of the country's greatest comedians. As a true professional, he is never wholly dependent upon a script and is master of the slick ad lib.

I remember an occasion when Arthur and I were appearing at the Connaught Rooms and a vocalist, whose spot number was the Cobbler's Song from *Chu Chin Chow*, said to us while waiting his call, 'Look, I've sung this song 2,345 times, how can I make it sound a bit different?'

'Try singing it with a mouthful of tacks,' was Arthur's quick quip.

To audiences he was and always will be known as 'Big-Hearted Arthur'. This was a schoolboy nickname which has always stuck. Every comedian hopes their public will laugh *with* them, but Arthur is one of the few who has never minded them laughing *at* him. He always got as much fun out of Dickie calling him a 'silly little man' as did the audience.

Arthur, like me, had no theatrical background and I believe his parents were quite horrified when he threw up his secure job as a clerk with Liverpool Corporation to join the 'Song

Salad' concert party in 1925 when any kind of job, especially one with a tasty pension at the end, was hard to get.

For years he trailed round the country with concert parties and in pantomime—for which he was a natural—during the winter. He was often featured in B.B.C. variety shows but remained what he called 'just a useful comedian' until he and Murdoch took the air with *Band Waggon* in January, 1938. That show did for Arthur what the *Garrison Theatre* did for me—sent him rocketing to the top and made his catch-phrases the coinage of listeners. More radio shows, films, television and stage work followed and I'm delighted that he won a courageous battle against a heart attack in 1967 and is today as sprightly, kindly and good humoured as he was during the days we were on the road together.

The spirit he showed in 1967 is typical of this great little man. He was knocking on sixty-four, and rehearsing for the London Palladium pantomime with all the fantastic energy he used to put into the Fol-de-Rols, when a trap-door—known in show business as the 'grave-trap'—collapsed beneath him. He sustained several cracked ribs and went off to Charing Cross Hospital for a pain-killing injection that would enable him not to miss the opening night.

The doctors were adamant that he should go home and rest. Two days later came the heart attack and Arthur was rushed to the intensive care unit at St George's Hospital. Even in these dire circumstances, as he was wheeled through the depressing hospital corridors, he says he quipped to the medical staff, 'I'm glad to see you've brought me the pretty way.' What a man!

Arthur and Dickie were perfect foils for each other—Arthur the little grimacing, bespectacled clown and Murdoch, tall, slim and handsome, letting his Charterhouse and Cambridge educational background show through.

After the war, during which he was a squadron leader in the R.A.F., Murdoch found further radio fame in *Much Binding in the Marsh*, a show about a mythical R.A.F. station. He was teamed with Kenneth Horne (who had been a R.A.F. wing commander) and the series ran until 1950. I may be prejudiced or perhaps a little too nostalgic but I always felt that the old *Band Waggon* show had the edge on *Much Binding in the Marsh.*

Unlike Arthur, Dickie didn't adjust readily to the expanding medium of television and although he was heard in endless radio shows and starred in many plays in London and the provinces, it was not until 1970 that he secured the success he deserved on the small screen.

David Frost invited Murdoch and Sam Costa (another 'Much Binding' character) to be guests on his Sunday night show, *That Was The Week That Was.* The viewers liked them so much that they were given a regular spot in the programme and won many new fans with their updated 'Much Binding' patter and songs.

To return to my concert-party days, I remember one disastrous occasion with the Fol-de-Rols when nothing seemed to go right from the moment we sang the opening chorus, 'You Can't Have Everything'. Murdoch edged up to me singing, 'I've left my props in the dressing-room,' and I replied vocally, 'I'll go and get them.'

It was my time for blushes later in the show. I was doing a number, 'Ma Pomme', with Arthur, Dickie and Walter Midgeley, the well-known tenor, when I realised as I left the stage that I had gone through the whole act with my flies undone. Had I realised it while I was on stage in that strictly non-permissive era, I'm sure I would have gone through the boards. It taught me a lesson never to go on stage or on a film set without, as they say, adjusting my clothing.

My three colleagues thought the incident too funny for words and that was my reaction years later when I heard of what occurred to Walter on a certain operatic occasion. The Yorkshire-born tenor achieved the rare distinction of singing the leading roles in many operas at Covent Garden.

On the night he was playing the Duke of Mantua in *Rigoletto* he opened his mouth wide for a deep breath before beginning his first big aria and managed to suck in half his false moustache, which stuck in his throat! The poor chap quickly turned his back on the audience, coughed up most of his whiskers, ripped off the other half of the moustache and finished the first act with a hairless top lip. After sipping some honey, and having a new moustache painted on during the interval, he was able to complete the role, although not without some discomfort. An examination by a throat specialist the following day produced an inch-long piece of nylon gauze, the moustache backing which had become lodged in the larynx.

Walter was a boon companion and shared my passion for snooker. During the fifties, when I did a lot of filming and he was singing at Covent Garden, we spent much of our leisure time in the mornings playing at a public house called 'The Greyhound' in Kensington Square.

With the Fol-de-Rols, we did two matinées and one evening show every day except Sundays. Mollie still continued her secretarial work in London and gradually, by pooling our cash, we managed to settle all the outstanding debts from my collapsed garage business.

Another outstanding Fol-de-Rols artiste was Gladys Merridew, the comedienne, who married Berhard Lee, best known to most of us as the Spymaster boss 'M' in the James Bond films. Bernard and Gladys had a lovely seventeenth-century cottage in the Kent village of Oare, and it was there she died tragically in a fire early in 1972. Bernard and Gladys were trapped in their bedroom when the fire started on the ground floor. Bernard escaped through a window and ran to get a ladder in an attempt to rescue Gladys but unhappily was unsuccessful. It was an awful end to a long and happy marriage.

As the 1938 season with the Hastings' company of the Fol-de-Rols came to an end I was on the look-out for a pianist to replace Jeff in my cabaret act and Elsie and Doris suggested that I should visit the Llandudno Company to hear a pianist called Bobby Alderson. A new partnership was established which still exists today and I hesitate to think of the thousands upon thousands of miles that Bobby and I have travelled entertaining people here and abroad.

It is certainly true to say that show business is like the curate's egg—good in parts. There is no joy and no money in 'resting' and just after Bobby joined me, I experienced a few of these enforced periods. I suppose the profession is no worse than some industries and commercial ventures except, perhaps, that a performer is much more at the mercy of the whim of the public. And in this connection it is worth remembering that while the most equable temperament is not always able to overcome sudden tensions the show business personality who allows his ego to become too inflated when he is bound for the top always dives to the bottom more swiftly and painfully when something goes wrong. People in this situation feel awfully lonely when they need a helping hand to haul them up again and none is forthcoming.

Happily, my lean period didn't last too long and strangely, although I had a pretty extensive repertoire of monologues, impressions and songs, it was my old stand-by gag of Max Miller doing an impersonation of Maurice Chevalier which brought me my first real solo success on radio in March, 1939. Also in that year, I first did the Professor Schtopundschtart monologue.

This character was supposed to be a German professor lecturing on such typically English subjects as football and cricket. The monologue clicked with the renowned B.B.C. producer, Leslie Bridgemont, who gave me the opportunity of broadcasting it from Newquay, Cornwall.

Leslie was a brilliant producer of major cabaret broadcasts from all parts of the country and I was sorry to hear of his death a few years ago. It is somewhat sad when a famous name no longer appears regularly in the *Radio Times* but Leslie and many other friends have special place among my memories.

Because of the success of the German professor, I decided to specialise for a time in doing impressions of people who had odd voices or peculiar ways of talking. One of my characters was based upon a commissionaire in the *Daily Express* office in Fleet Street. He was such a true Cockney that he practically swallowed his words.

One day when I was leaving Broadcasting House with Dickie Murdoch, I had to step over the legs of a couple of fellows who were sitting in the sunshine with their backs against the wall eating their lunches from paper bags. As we passed, I heard one say to the other, 'I don't know what my old woman has given me for dinner today, but I didn't oughter 'ave et it.'

I remarked to Dickie, 'If that isn't the cue for a song I don't know what is. . . .' It became one of my most popular numbers and I think provided me with the first catch-phrase to be picked up by members of the public.

Here is the opening verse:

I'm a funny kinda fellah in a funny kinda way,
I don't mean laughin' funny, I mean peculiar as they say.
I'm what my friends and relatives call rather weak inside
And although I know I've got ter eat, some food I can't abide.
I had some jam on kippers once and had to go to bed,
And when the doctor he came round what do you think he said?
Well, you didn't oughter 'ave et it, that's what the doctor said.
I didn't oughter 'ave et it, I answered from my bed.
He said, you do that again I'm sure you will regret it,
Eating jam on kippers, nah, you didn't oughter 'ave et it. . . .

The audiences of those days loved it and invariably joined in with 'you didn't oughter 'ave et it'.

Then I heard about a man who was known as a wheel-tapper. He walked up and down the railway lines tapping train wheels and rails until he won a packet on the football pools and went right up in the world. He gave up his job but still talked about it saying, 'walkin' hup hand dahn the rawlway lanes . . .' This was a slice of his true Cockney accent somewhat strangely welded to a piece of the Mayfair drawl.

I wrote a monologue about him which ended with the following verse:

> So now the station's closed and I just live a life of ease,
> But if ever for a change my soul it pines,
> I climb hup in the signal box and listen to the whistles
> While the trains run hup hand dahn the rawlway lanes.

I had written about four verses of this song when I became completely stuck and tossed it on one side—very close to the wastepaper basket! Mollie picked it up, handed it to me and said, 'Finish it, Jack. I think an audience will like it.'

I took her advice and about two weeks later, I was asked to do a five-minute spot in the radio show *Monday Night at Eight* which was produced by the late Harry S. Pepper and Ronnie Waldman. When it came to my turn for rehearsal, Charlie Shadwell and his band had disappeared for cups of tea (or perhaps a glass of something a little stronger and more interesting!). I decided, however, to chance my arm and do the 'rawlway' number although I had little confidence in the number and thought it sounded a bit daft. There was nobody about and I had my back to the control room. I turned to Bobby Alderson and said, 'Let's give it a go, Bobby.' We did just that and when we had finished and walked away from the piano, we suddenly saw Harry, Ronnie and Doris Arnold, who had been in the control room all the time, bursting with merriment. When they learned I had written the thing they asked for as many more like it as I could produce.

Undoubtedly, what was funny yesteryear is not necessarily so today, but nevertheless whenever I make stage appearances before audiences who remember the pre-war and wartime broadcasts I have requests for that old number.

Another one many people have not forgotten is 'My Brother in the Life Guards', which was about a chap who was terribly proud of his brother who rode a mare called Edna. The last verse was:

> Well I think I've told you quite enough about my brother Sid,
> I could go on talking all night long, you'd get fed up if I did.

But if ever you go down Whitehall and you've got some time
to spare,
And you see two blokes on horseback on the right from Trafalgar Square,
And one of them has a shiny nose and he's on a jet black mare,
Well, that's Edna and my brother in the Life Guards. . . .

Business became brisker and I began to repeat my success in cabaret. By 1939 B.B.C. bookings were quite heavy. Dear old Jeff's 'The Legionnaires' song provided the title for a show in which I appeared as a Cockney—not at all difficult considering the place of my birth!

On many occasions, I was lucky enough to appear in the B.B.C.'s *All-Star Music Hall* with top-liners like Ben Lyon and Bebe Daniels.

It was in the summer of 1939, too, that I appeared professionally for the second time with my sisters, Elsie and Doris. I was billed as Jack Warner and it was still not generally known that I was a brother of the famous Gert and Daisy. The three of us were with a concert party booked for a week at 'The Sparrow's Nest', Lowestoft, at the end of August. We did the show for the first half of the week, but when we went to the theatre to collect our mail on the Thursday morning we found that the place had been commandeered by the Royal Navy.

I am not unduly superstitious but on that day there was a terrible thunderstorm and I experienced an acute sense of impending disaster. There had been, of course, talk of war for some time but like so many others, I was confident that a head-on clash with Germany would be averted. I realised that my optimism was completely unjustified when we walked into the navy that day.

The previous week I had been in a show at Huddersfield and the fear of war so gripped the people there that I had to ask the meagre audience, who had left the security of their homes, to sit together in the first two rows. I did my usual act but it really was one of the most melancholy appearances I have ever made.

By the time we had returned to London, war had been declared. The black-out was upon us and London had become a dead city with its inhabitants and commuters anxiously waiting to see what next would occur.

So far as the nation's affairs were concerned, Mollie and I were no worse off than anybody else, but the situation was terribly disheartening because we had just overcome the financial problems which had haunted us for several years and now the prospects of employment in show business looked as bright as the corroded button on a soldier's greatcoat.

Aged forty-four in 1939, I was well over the limit for military service but in view of my Royal Flying Corps experience in World War I, I thought the R.A.F. might decide that I could be useful to them. I bowled along to the recruiting depot and saw the queues of bright young chaps eager to fly and I can't say I was surprised when the recruiting sergeant indicated that he regarded me as a somewhat over-enthusiastic veteran. Nevertheless, I knew that my experience in the motor industry could be of some value to the country, but what I could not decide was whether it outweighed whatever talent I possessed for show business.

The B.B.C. had moved its headquarters to Bristol and was relaying recorded broadcasts only so that the chance of an early job with the Corporation appeared remote. The war was six weeks old when I learned that the B.B.C. was about to sign up artistes for live broadcasts that were shortly to be resumed. Ever the opportunist, I sent a telegram to Arthur Brown, then booking manager: 'Any chance for me?—Jack Warner'.

I wasn't in a financial position to send a wordy wire and, frankly, I didn't really expect to be taken on, but by return I had a telegram offering me fifteen guineas for two shows. Little did Brown realise that I was in such a sorry state that I would have done, three shows for five guineas. Fifteen represented riches.

The following week, I went to Bristol on my own and did the two broadcasts and I was then asked to do a couple more. It was plain sailing afterwards with a regular two shows a week routine.

I rented a little room—ten bob a week—at the top of Blackboys Hill, Bristol, and it was within those four walls that I disciplined myself to write new material.

Some little time before I clinched the arrangement with the B.B.C., Mollie was introduced in London to a lady clairvoyant who, not surprisingly, seemed keen to tell her fortune. Mollie was not a great believer in the prophetic and neither was I and she accepted the offer lightheartedly. She was more than a little surprised when she was told, 'You and your husband have been having a bad time lately, but I can tell you that all your problems will soon vanish. I can see a big hall, I can hear music and there are hundreds of people clapping and cheering. It will all happen within five weeks and you will have no further worries.'

It seemed a very unlikely prediction at the time, but exactly five weeks later it began to justify itself.

At the end of November I was walking along Whiteladies Road when Charlie Shadwell, by then director of the B.B.C. Variety Orchestra, emerged from the corporation's temporary headquarters. He told me that the B.B.C. had just accepted his idea for a new version of a show called *Garrison Theatre* which he had staged for the troops during the 1914–18 war.

'I was hoping that I would be able to contact you,' said Charlie, 'because we want someone to play a Cockney soldier who makes daft remarks and keeps interrupting the show. I think you're made for the part. How about it?'

How about it! For me a fairy had waved a magic wand. I couldn't start rehearsals quickly enough and was more thrilled by the prospects than I could ever remember before when the show was broadcast on December 9th, 1939.

I shall always be grateful to Charlie because he gave me the opportunity which I had dreamed of for so many years—a regular spot in a regular show and a regular meal ticket. Later I was to top the bill at the London Palladium in *Garrison Theatre!*

Charlie, who plays the piano, organ and violin, had trained at the Royal Academy of Music and was musical director of the Coventry Hippodrome Orchestra before he joined the B.B.C. After launching and piloting *Garrison Theatre* through the early days of the war, Charlie made an even greater name for himself—or perhaps it would be more accurate to say that he became more of a character to the listening public—when he directed the orchestra for *ITMA*. Audiences loved his fast cross-talk with Tommy Handley and Charlie's incredible laugh was utterly infectious. He resigned from the B.B.C. in 1946 to take his own twenty-one piece orchestra on tour and was an enormous success.

Some years later he bought the six-hundred-year-old pub, 'The Green Man', at Trumpington, near Cambridge. We renewed our happy association and re-lived some memorable situations when I went to Cambridge not long ago to give a show in aid of the Police Dependents' Trust. The magnificent laugh and good humour remain and his popularity as mine host is unrivalled.

A story about a band leader Charlie engaged to play at a seaside resort is still fresh in my mind: Charlie received this wire from the poor chap: 'Pier burning. Piano in sea. Please wire instructions.'

Charlie replied, 'Keep the home fires burning. Hire diver to tune piano.'

That kind of repartee from this talented musician did much to boost the morale of many people during the dark war years.

Of course, *Garrison Theatre* was not a theatre at all but the Clifton Parish Hall on the outskirts of Bristol. We even lacked a real stage. A small space in the hall was cleared for the microphones and artists, with the orchestra raised on a small dais at the rear. Outside the hall, a board gave details of Bible classes and Sunday school meetings and inside there was an Air Raid Precautions notice informing us that we could go to the church crypt in the event of a raid.

Troops were invited to see the show and when they clumped

into the tiny hall in their heavy studded boots the noise was deafening. Harry Pepper, the producer, kept everything well under control with his first call of, 'Quiet everybody, please!' He told the lads to join in the choruses when the broadcast was on, but warned them that anyone singing rude versions of any of the songs would be thrown out!

The show's name was taken from that of an actual theatre—the Garrison Theatre, Ripon, Yorkshire—where Charlie Shadwell had staged the World War I entertainment. A lieutenant in the West Yorkshire Regiment, he had been invalided home from France and sent to the Northern Command depot at Ripon in charge of troop entertainment. Almost every famous artiste of the time played there.

He and Harry Pepper successfully re-created this wartime theatre atmosphere and the presence of genuine troops proved a big asset because having exchanged the cold and unfriendly confines of barracks for the simulated warmth of a temporary theatre, and the rigorous parade ground discipline for the comedians' cracks, they were in a relaxed mood that guaranteed every performer an enthusiastic reception.

Few members of the audience and hardly a listener knew that the irascible sergeant major in the show was the genuine article—Regimental Sergeant-Major Filtness, who had been Shadwell's sergeant-major during World War I. At the age of fifty-one he had rejoined the army, but had permission to fulfil his B.B.C. contract. His booming voice made a terrific impression.

I gave a lot of thought to my characterisation of the Cockney private. When I wrote my material, I tried to live up to my personal show business slogan—try to do something that hasn't been done before. Sitting in my little attic room, I dreamed up the idea of letters from a fictitious brother, Sid.

The very first *Garrison Theatre* show was running a bit late and somebody in the control room crept into the hall and whispered in my ear, 'Mr. Pepper says do the monologue but cut out the letter from brother Sid.' I took a chance and did the opposite—and Sid was born. I had little idea how famous he would become during those war years.

Only recently a lady stopped me and told me how much her son had enjoyed the *Garrison Theatre* shows and particularly the letters from Sid. 'My son was killed in the Battle of Britain,' she told me, 'but every time I think of him I think of you.'

The punch line to these letters was always in the postscript and I made a guess at those which had been the favourites with this lady's son. She was delighted when I picked on these two:

'P.S. I can't tell you where I am, but if Hitler invades us we shall pelt him with Margate rock. . . .'

'P.S. I thought I was coming home on leave this week, but Lord Gort thought different. . . .'

I was very touched to think that after more than thirty years those postscripts still meant something to someone, and I shall ever be grateful to Charlie Shadwell for giving me an opportunity to bring some cheer to the nation at a time when everyone desperately needed to laugh about something. Psychologically it was right for me and the British public. Sometimes, in my leisure moments, I look through some of the faded letters I received from listeners and servicemen and women telling me how much they had enjoyed the entertainment. Those old letters make me feel extremely humble and never fail to bring a lump to my throat.

Most comedians had their catch-phrases then as now and I had several. There was, 'Vereee good, sir,' 'Blue pencil' and, of course, 'Mind my bike!' The last one, as with most, owed its existence to chance. I was constantly trying to think up new gags to herald my entrance to the show. One week, I was supposed to come up through the orchestra; another time down through the wings and once was supposed to be helping the electrician to put bulbs in footlights. The small things stick in my mind—remembering that the show was heard and not seen, except by the tiny audience in the parish hall—and that there was no stage and of course no footlights. We spent a lot of time trying to discover how it would sound if light bulbs were dropped—as they were assumed to be—by me, the awkward soldier. The sound which emerges from the radio at home does not always match the sound made into the microphone and to complicate matters yet further, we certainly couldn't waste good light bulbs during the austere wartime days. Eventually we achieved the right effect by making popping noises with cardboard boxes but it took us ages to perfect the sound.

The week after the bulb incident, Harry Pepper asked me how I planned to make my entrance. I had to confess that I was running out of ideas but I told him I had thought of something that would either go very well or prove to be the daftest thing I'd ever done.

I said that I wanted the listeners to imagine that I was riding down through the stalls on a bicycle and ringing the bell. Harry didn't bat an eyelid. He just said, 'Good! I've got a bell and hooter in the prop box.'

There can be few people who listened to those broadcasts who don't remember the 'Mind my bike' phrase. In show business you can write something you think will make people fall about in helpless laughter and it surprises the artist by expiring on delivery, while a simple remark can be interpreted as inexpressibly funny.

When I dropped the phrase for two weeks, I had three thousand letters from listeners asking why. The only complaint came from a father who wrote, 'I am very keen on your *Garrison Theatre* show and I like the comedy very much, but I have spent several hundreds of pounds on my son's education and all he can do is shout 'Mind my bike' in a very raucous Cockney voice. I'm trying to break him of the habit so will you please stop saying it?'

The phrases received recognition in some odd places. At a London police court a constable gave evidence about stopping Mr. Warner, a lorry driver. The magistrate asked, 'Did he ask you what the blue pencil you wanted?' and seemed almost disappointed when the officer replied, 'No sir, this was a different Warner.'

Charlie Shadwell was fined at Bristol for causing an obstruction with his car. His solicitor said, 'Mr. Shadwell became engrossed in conversation with Mr. Jack Warner . . . they were discussing that gentleman's bicycle, about which you have no doubt heard.'

The monologues and songs were picked up by cartoonists and even by Ivor Brown, a Fleet Street notability and critic, who favoured me with a double-column feature headed 'The Nation and Its Noises', in which he wrote, 'The Saturday nights of the nation have been rendered more agreeable of late by the presence of Mr. Jack Warner in the broadcasts of *Garrison Theatre*. What Mr. Warner says is not, when one reads it or its kind in cold print, particularly funny, but he makes it seem so.'

Mr. Brown went on to say that I shared, with some other B.B.C. stars, 'that mysterious and most profitable possession—a radio personality. . . . The Private Warner of *Garrison Theatre* is one of those who are somehow seen as well as definitely heard and, of course, to see him even with the mind's eye is to love him. . . .'

The 'cod' lecture is an old plot in entertainment and I found they went down very well over the air, especially one in which I impersonated a Cockney character who kept his eels in fish tanks. It was introduced thus: 'Good evening one and all. Tonight I would like to give you a talk on my charges which are ills. I will repeat that—ills.

'Now there's all kinds of ills, fresh water ills, salt water ills and conger ills. These latter bein' outsize and what is commonly known as whoppers. Now 'ave you ever tried to catch a rill slippery ill? If you 'ave not, practise in your wash'and basin with a piece of rill slippery soap and you will find that the rill slippery soap will fill like a rill slippery ill and fill very rill.

'Sometimes, to escape your notice, ills 'ide. They 'ide under pieces of rock, stone or 'ard wood, but if you wish to find them do not despair because all you 'ave to do is lift the rock, stone or 'ard wood and there, to your amazed gaze, the little ill stands revilled. . . .'

I knocked out this nonsense when travelling by train from Waterloo to Bournemouth to do a broadcast. It was rubbish really but I delivered this lecture over the air that evening and from that moment, everyone began talking about having rill mills. It was the sheer topicality of the expression that made the public catch on to it. A real meal in those days of austerity was a dream of the past. The Ministry of Agriculture played an unwitting part in popularising the dotty phrase when they issued an official leaflet pointing out the food value of eels. It was inevitable that alert sub-editors on national newspapers should produce headlines like, 'Ills are rill Mills'.

Of course, as a Cockney, I was well equipped to exploit the idiom, but fellow Cockneys, who knew no other way of expressing themselves, could see little humour in it. I have always been passionately fond of eels and the late Bob Cook, a well-known eel pie merchant in London, had been one of my friends for many many years. I met him soon after I had delivered the eel keeper's lecture and he said, 'You're doing well on the old wireless, Jack, but tell me, what's all this lark about ills? Everybody know there's all kinds of ills.' My jargon was, in fact, his everyday talk.

I received a great deal of help from Harry Pepper during the *Garrison Theatre* days. I had known him before the programme was devised because for several years he had played the piano for his father, Will Pepper, the owner and producer of a seaside concert party called 'The White Coons'. I was introduced to him when Elsie and Doris were appearing with the show at Clacton. Harry wrote many of the numbers for the concert party and, in fact, composed several really famous songs. Many people think that 'Carry Me Back to Green Green Pastures' is a traditional negro spiritual, but both music and lyrics were written by Harry. He joined the B.B.C in 1932 and he was the man who first thought up the idea of a radio minstrel show—the famous *Kentucky Minstrels*. It could be said that the *Black and White Minstrel Show*, now world famous, is a direct descendant of the old radio programme.

Harry was one of the corporation's top producers, and in addition to *Garrison Theatre*, he was responsible for *Band Waggon*, *Hi Gang!* and *Monday Night at Eight*, which ran for twelve years. This last programme provides a glorious example of how a broadcasting error can be turned into an asset by somebody as astute as Harry.

In one of the early broadcasts, a really ghastly mistake occurred and, as is customary, listeners rushed to their telephones to complain while the show was still on the air. However, they were completely deceived when Harry closed the programme by saying, 'I wonder how many of you were clever enough to spot my deliberate mistake . . .?' His cunning evasion of an for apology the error on this occasion led to the inclusion of a deliberate mistake in all ensuing programmes which listeners were invited to spot!

Harry married pianist Doris Arnold who for years presented a popular record programme of serious music under the title of 'Those You Have Loved'. They were very happily married and it was a terrible shock to Pep—as we all called him—when Doris died suddenly in 1969. He didn't struggle on long without her and less than a year later he, too, had died.

I was delighted that I was given the opportunity to express my gratitude to Harry Pepper, who helped to make me a star, when he was the victim—and that's how I see all of them—of one of Eamonn Andrews' *This Is Your Life* programmes. He was terribly thrilled to find himself surrounded by the old team of Charlie Shadwell, Arthur Askey, Richard Murdoch, Ben Lyon and Vic Oliver.

My story of *Garrison Theatre* would be incomplete if I didn't refer to one of the most popular characters with the troops, my 'littel gel'—Joan Winters—with whom I used to exchange saucy chat. Joan was actually Charlie's daughter and she really was a little girl, very small and neat, with lovely auburn hair and possessing the same infectious laugh as her father. She had a colossal fan mail from the boys in the services, who asked for dates and sent her proposals of marriage.

I was best man at her wedding in Edinburgh to Jack Venables, who worked for the London Petroleum Board. At that time, *Garrison Theatre* was touring and we were due in Newcastle that evening. Once again, my driving ability proved more than useful and I managed to get the newly-weds to Newcastle just in time for Joan to appear on stage as the curtain went up. Unfortunately, the marriage didn't endure and following a divorce in 1948, Joan married Guy Fielding, with whom she teamed up in a comedy–singing–dancing duo. They did well in this country and overseas and are now living and working in America.

I have often thought that if I hadn't become an actor I would have enjoyed being an osteopath because they can achieve so much. I have had a lot of experiences with them and my first was in 1939 when I was introduced to a man named John Hancock. I was in trouble with my right foot and, in fact, I couldn't even walk on it. I had been told about Hancock and went to see him. He examined my foot and said he thought he could help me. 'How long?' I asked. 'In about ten minutes,' he replied. And that is literally how long it took him to put my metatarsal joint back into place. Then he bound my foot and told me to stand on it. I did just that and was able to walk normally. To me that was a near miracle.

Another time John Hancock helped me was when I was on the halls with *Garrison Theatre*. If I have a cold it always affects my throat and when it does I lose my voice. If I lost my voice permanently, of course I should lose my living, so I am naturally careful about my health. On this occasion, just before the second house at Finsbury Park Empire, I realised that my voice was fast disappearing and I became really worried. I had croaked my way through the first house and knew that the worst thing I could do would be to continue using my voice. But I was due on stage again in half an hour and did not want to disappoint the audience. As luck would have it John Hancock and his wife had arrived to see the show and he came round to me in my dressing room. He undid the collar of my battledress uniform and fiddled around with my throat until I heard and felt something like a click. Then on John's instructions I gargled with a weak solution of vinegar and water and, believe it or not, I was on stage shortly afterwards shouting so loudly that I think the other members of the cast suspected me of kidding them during the first house, but if John hadn't been there to see the show I would have been out of the cast for the rest of the week.

It's a strange thing but some doctors will not accept osteopathy at any price and often those who do keep quiet about it. A medical student starts his work by studying a plastic skeleton because that is literally the bones of the business. Obviously if a bone is displaced it has to be put back. To ignore the bones is rather like having something wrong with the brakes of a car and saying, 'Put some oil in the engine.' I've knocked myself about a bit from time to time and whenever I have displaced a bone it has always been an osteopath who has put it right.

Sometimes a bit of luck can achieve what medical assistance has failed to do. An example that comes to my mind is the case of Joe Waters (he has my legal name but is not related), the producer of Dixon on television. A few years ago he was in a serious car accident and was more or less chair-bound, although he continued to work for the B.B.C. He was always very meticulous about detail and would run a check himself before being satisfied. In one Dixon episode there was a scene in which a crowd of women on a coach trip to Southend were called upon to go down a helter-skelter. Joe, with his usual care and despite his physical handicap, decided that he must first test the slide. He got on at the top and went whizzing down, but couldn't stop himself and banged into a wall at the bottom. He was picked up and taken home, where he remained in bed for a couple of days. Joe then decided that he'd got to try moving around again and rather dubiously got out of bed. To his absolute amazement he found he could walk quite normally. His doctor exclaimed, 'This is quite fantastic.

All those bound-up muscles and lesions that were stopping you from walking properly have been put right by the knock you took. I don't know exactly what you did, but whatever it was has put you on your feet again.' It is what we at *Dixon of Dock Green* called the Joe Waters miracle, because it really is miraculous when you cure yourself by accident.

During *Garrison Theatre* days, I added yet another dimension to my show business career. The B.B.C. began to present radio versions of musical films and I learned that *The Love Parade* was one that would be broadcast. Maurice Chevalier was invited to play his original role but couldn't make it and the whole project began to flounder. I went to the studios one day and saw John Watt, the producer. I asked him if he would like to hear a little French record I had made and he agreed to listen. He was surprised to learn that I could speak fluent French and even more surprised when he heard the record.

'Is that really you?' he asked.

'It is indeed,' I said.

'Well I'm damned. You can take Maurice's part.'

The show was presented on February 9th, 1940, and I played opposite Anne Ziegler, famous partner of Webster Booth. Anne took the original role played by film star Jeanette MacDonald. Working with Anne was a memorable experience. Apart from having a splendid voice, she had a wonderful sense of humour and a sweet temperament.

I had never envisaged myself in a musical and was astonished to receive congratulatory telegrams from all over the world. I think that probably, because of my Cockney part in the *Garrison Theatre* shows, I had become typed in the minds of many listeners who were astonished that I could sing and act.

In April, 1940, as the phoney war drew ever nearer to becoming a real war, I was asked if I would go to Paris with E.N.S.A. to take part in a show at the Opera House. I didn't think I was ready to play in such a plush setting and before an audience largely made up of sophisticated Parisiennes. I could say 'Mind my bike' in England as many times as I wished and raise a laugh but it wouldn't have meant a damned thing to a French audience. But then I learned that Maurice Chevalier was to appear in the show and I couldn't resist the opportunity of being with him on the same bill.

The stage of the opera house is the largest in the world and resembled a massive covered-in park. On the night I stood in the wings I was completely petrified and gradually became fearful that my legs wouldn't obey orders and carry me into the pool of light. Suddenly, though, I felt a tap on my shoulder and heard that unmistakable voice, 'Don't worry, Jack. Good luck!'

Those comforting words from Maurice the master caused my panic to evaporate. I sang my version of the hit tune 'Boom' without a tremor of nervousness, because from the corner of my eye I could see Maurice standing in the wings all through the number. I have never in my long life-span met a more charming man.

The show was a combined Anglo-French effort to raise money to provide huts for Allied troops in France and M. Paul Reynaud, the President, was among the many dignitaries present on that memorable evening. Gracie Fields shared the top billing with Maurice and she was in great form. The programme was broadcast to Britain but I later learned that reception was very poor and was faded out on the dot of 10 p.m. because the B.B.C. had to change wavelengths.

Everyone present that night would have been truly shattered had they known that within months Paris would be under the domination of the hated Nazis. The very purpose of the show depressingly illustrated the unpreparedness for war of both Britain and France.

The *Garrison Theatre* radio show ended the following month —in May, 1940—and it was taken over by Jack Hylton, one of the foremost of London's impressarios. Shortly before war was declared, he had presented *Band Waggon*, with Askey and Murdoch, at the London Palladium, and he lined up the *Garrison Theatre* for his next major production there. We gave a week's show at Brighton, which was really a run-up to our opening at the Palladium where we stayed for four-and-a-half months before going on tour in the provinces.

On the stage we all wore uniforms appropriate to our supposed rank and even the orchestral members and the theatre staff were in khaki. The show was presented with a second proscenium on the stage, with seats reserved for servicemen who were ushered in as they arrived.

One night, soldiers who only that morning had been evacuated from Dunkirk were shown to their seats. Those who organised the visit were motivated only by kindness, but I felt that perhaps it was somewhat misplaced. The faces of those boys were etched with bewilderment and in some instances sheer horror. It was hoped that our humour and good spirits would overcome their distress but recalling the bloody sights I myself had witnessed in World War I, I realised that our guests were still in shock, and if their minds registered anything at all, it was the memory of the dead comrades they had left behind.

Like all artistes who attempted to bring some bright patches to the lives of the fighting men, I often found myself the recipient of their stories. I think that in those days of tragedy and heartbreak the boys found it comforting to express their feelings to somebody like me who was a civilian and something of a father figure. One young lad called to see me at the end of the show on the first day of the Dunkirk evacuation and told me how much he had enjoyed the performance adding, 'I'm jolly lucky to be here tonight. The boat I was in was sunk and all my mates drowned.'

I invited him to visit us again backstage as soon as he could, and I saw him again while we were on tour. We chatted in my dressing room and I told him I would leave tickets at the box-office for him and his wife at the end of the week. On the Saturday night I received a little pencilled note, 'Sorry I can't come tonight. My brother in the R.A.F. was killed yesterday.' Then there was Mary, a beautiful raven-haired W.A.A.F. officer who had seen our show in Brighton and visited the

Palladium with her husband, Bill, a pilot officer. They had married that morning. He was shot down and killed twenty-four hours later.

A sergeant in the Royal Corps of Signals made three trips to the Palladium because he was crazy about *Garrison Theatre*. The fourth time he came we were playing in Manchester, which was his home city. He was minus his right arm—lost in a London air-raid.

I could fill this book with stories of human misery, which all of us in show business during the war had to thrust from our minds. Nobody could afford to yield to depression. Our job was to try and spread a little cheer—not gloom.

This was my intention as I waited in the wings to make my entrance one night at a Glasgow theatre. Suddenly I felt a faint movement behind me and a voice muttered, 'Sing "Auld Lang Syne" when you get out there.'

'I'm here to sing "If You Were the Only Girl in the World",' I said to my unseen intruder, 'and we can't make changes at the last moment even if the band could play it.'

It was not a very flattering comment on the orchestra's ability, but frankly, I didn't know what to say in this ugly situation.

'Well, they'd bloody well better learn because I want you to sing "Auld Lang Syne".'

I swung round as I heard the click of a knife to face a drunken sailor brandishing a formidable weapon, but a well-built Royal Navy petty officer saw him at the same time, rushed over and floored him with a powerful uppercut that put an end to the argument.

Of course, before *Garrison Theatre* reached the end of its run at the Palladium, we were in the midst of the air-raids. When the bombs were dropping I used to go on to the stage sometimes for as long as an hour to keep the ball rolling with jokes and monologues until the sound of the bombers receded into the night. The audiences were absolutely wonderful and there was never any panic. It was the same in the provinces.

We were at the Palace in Manchester for three weeks where we put on two afternoon shows so that the audience had a chance of reaching their homes before the night raids started. Because of the nature of my job I was allowed to use my car, a Rover 10, and while we were playing Manchester, I drove to London to take part in a special Sunday night gala concert for the troops. I stayed overnight and started the 184-mile trip back to Manchester the following morning. All went well until I reached a village just beyond Stafford, when the dynamo bracket broke. The local garage was closed so I knocked up the proprietor. He was not too concerned about my problem. 'Can't do anything now, I'm having my dinner,' he said.

I explained why I had to be in Manchester by the early afternoon and asked if I could use his garage and tools. He shrugged, 'Help yourself.' I welded the bracket, got back into the car and broke every rule of the road to arrive at the Palace just a minute before I was due on the stage. My legs were shaking when I reached my dressing room, where I donned my battledress and without any make-up hurried on to the stage just as the orchestra was playing my music.

Sometimes, show business people realise they are not as famous as they imagine themselves to be. When we were working in Newcastle, I decided to look up an old chum called Murray, who was in the motor car business. He seemed pleased enough to see me and we exchanged the usual pleasantries, but he told me he had little time to spare as he had to rush out to buy tickets for *Garrison Theatre*. But he did invite me to join his party at the show, until it dawned on him that I was the Jack Warner he was anxious to see.

It was November, 1941, before we completed our provincial tour and Jack Hylton booked the show at the Coliseum for a six-week season. I was pleased to be back in London again—despite aid-raids. At the end of the tour, the cast clubbed together and bought me a wallet in baby crocodile skin to mark the occasion of the show's 1,000th performance. On our first night at the Coliseum, I left the wallet in my dressing room and during a moment when the entire cast was on stage, some toe-rag nicked it.

The theft was as ironic as any that occurred in a *Dixon of Dock Green* episode, since the show was a special one put on for the police and was attended by the King of Sweden, Mr. Herbert Morrison, then Home Secretary, Sir Edward Evans, Scotland Yard's top brass and two thousand other coppers. Some time later, a police officer called at my home to return my driving licence and ration book—but no wallet!

Jack Hylton was a very tough boss and a strict disciplinarian. He believed in self-discipline and expected those who worked for him to do likewise. He was a perfectionist, demanded as much from others, and had no time for failures. If a show he presented was not an immediate success, he would close it at the end of the week—and have its successor ready by the Monday!

There is a story that Hylton arrived in London from his native Lancashire with only a shilling in his pocket. I'm prepared to believe it because he was the sort of bloke who could make a fortune from a shilling. He came up the hard way, playing the piano and clog dancing in his father's public house in Bolton when he was only ten years old.

From that early beginning, he moved on, becoming a pianist at pierrot shows and in the type of cinemas that were known in those days as flea pits. His first London job was as a cinema organist in Stoke Newington, where he played appropriate musical accompaniments to silent films. By 1913 he was playing the piano at one of London's first night clubs, but it took him ten years to reach the West End—in the band at the Queen's Hall Roof night club.

It was about this time, in the middle twenties, that a new type of dance music was catching on—the big band sound, imported from America on gramophone records. Hylton, who, as I came to realise, had an uncanny knack of knowing what the public wanted even before they knew themselves, decided that this brand of cleverly orchestrated twentieth-century music was here to stay. He formed his own band and for the next fifteen years, Jack Hylton's Dance Orchestra was as famous as any other in the world. They made a highly successful tour of Europe and were no less popular in Britain for their recordings and broadcasts.

When I first met him in 1940, Hylton had not long forsaken the conductor's rostrum for his new role of theatrical impresario. In fact, *Band Waggon* was the first radio show he booked for the stage, with *Garrison Theatre* providing him with his second success. From that time onwards, he presented anything that he believed would 'go', from the Crazy Gang in the West End to the London Philharmonic Orchestra in a tour of variety theatres—to prevent its dissolution. Heaven knows how many shows he put on but I recall *Call Me Madam*, *Kiss Me Kate*, *Pal Joey* and *Kismet* among the spectacular musicals, and *Anna Lucasta* and *The Moon Is Blue* among the straight plays.

Jack brought Ingrid Bergman to England to play Joan of Arc and presented both the Italian tenor Gigli and Maurice Chevalier in programmes in which they had the stage to themselves. When he died—following a heart attack at the age of seventy-two in 1965—his name was still in lights in the West End—above the musical, *Camelot*, at Drury Lane. What a man! He had been at the top one way or another for forty years.

I recall sitting with him in the stalls during a period when it was rather difficult to recruit suitable girls for the chorus. Two came on to the stage and with some asperity, Jack muttered 'Oh, they're bringing on the barmaids now, are they?'

In fact, the two girls, who were sisters, were well worth watching and certainly didn't deserve Jack's stricture. I was in Somerset in 1973 and met one of them, Irene Mitchell, now the head of the Beckery Training Centre for Mentally Handicapped Children near Glastonbury. She never married or became famous or rich but she has happy memories of her days with *Garrison Theatre*. She is certainly doing a fine job in helping children unable to help themselves.

During my long stint with *Garrison Theatre*, my sisters did a lot of broadcasting—but not always for money. The first broadcasts ever 'donated' by variety artists to a government department were those given by Elsie and Doris (as Gert and Daisy, of course) for the wartime Ministry of Food.

They did a radio spot every evening after the six o'clock news, talking about how to get the best value out of what money and coupons could secure. They were great ones for doing something for nothing and helping people whenever they could.

Their fame by that time had spread abroad and two aeroplanes used in the fierce battles that took place over the George Cross island of Malta had been christened 'Gert' and 'Daisy'—so were two elephants at the London Zoo! After the war, my sisters were awarded the O.B.E.

For everybody in the business, touring during the war was pretty tough. Trains were often delayed for one reason or another—not least by the bombing raids. A lack of staff backstage often presented problems.

Throughout our lives, Elsie, Doris and I have always maintained our close family ties and nobody was more delighted and thrilled than were my sisters when, after a protracted struggle, I managed to haul myself to the top. I have explained earlier why I felt it necessary to change my name and I must admit that there have been occasions when it has caused some confusion.

In 1944, my sisters went to India to give concerts to the troops. When they arrived, they were greeted by a young naval lieutenant who said that he had been assigned to them as escort and general factotum.

'Oh good,' said the girls, 'and what's your name?'

'Jack Warner,' he replied.

'Now just listen to him. . . .'

'I'm sorry,' said the sailor, 'but that is my real name.' Maybe his commanding officer had a sense of humour when he detailed the chap for that particular job, or maybe he knew that the young officer was keen to get into show business. Anyway,

Elsie and Doris told him to look me up when the war was over and he did just that—arriving at Lime Grove studios when I was making the film *Holiday Camp.*

I was a little bewildered over the question of his monniker and when I mentioned it to him he said, 'Well, that's the size of it. I can't very well take your name away from you after all this time but I don't know what else I can call myself.'

I suggested that he might like to become 'John Warren' and he readily agreed. He got a start in television commercials and appeared so often in one particular advertisement that he found he was recognised wherever he went. He then discovered he possessed a talent for writing and has been exploiting this ever since. John Warren has produced scripts for comedians in the Dick Emery bracket—and you can't do better than that!

I was also often confused with the great Hollywood film magnate, Jack Warner, and for several years, I received Christmas cards from the Aga Khan at my home in Kent which I re-directed to the Hollywood Warner.

When he was involved in a serious car accident, scores of people telephoned me to sympathise. I can't imagine what gave them the idea that I was driving around America in high-powered roadsters.

We continued with *Garrison Theatre* until July, 1942, making two and three returns to some theatres where we were very popular. When my 'littel gel', Joan Winters, left to have a baby, that gigantic man, Bryan Michie (he was all of twenty stone), joined us as compere. He wore the uniform of an A.T.S. private and became 'the littel gel' much to the delight of audiences up and down the country.

Within a week of *Garrison Theatre* folding, we were touring in another Hylton production, *Piccadilly Playtime.* In this show, Bryan had a spot called 'Stars of Tomorrow'—a talent competition. We were playing at Morecambe Winter Gardens when he introduced two promising newcomers in a song, dance and cross-talk act—two lads called Eric Morecambe and Ernie Wise, both aged sixteen!

Hereabouts, Bobby Alderson was called up for military service and as he had been taking part in a sketch I was doing called 'The Plumber's Mate' we were in a bit of a jam. Then somebody suggested we should stick a moustache on Ernie Wise and let him play the part. At sixteen years of age, Ernie was a bit too youthful, but we thought we might get away with it because the pair of them had come up damned well with their song and dance act, and if they were nervous, they certainly hadn't shown it.

I went on first to do my solo spot and had a bit of a rough opening with a woman, who was well pickled, shouting and playing merry hell. I went to the end of the stage and told her to behave herself or I would have the curtain pulled down. She quietened down and a few minutes later we presented the sketch. This went smoothly enough until Ernie appeared with his false moustache. It provided a cue for our boozed interrupter. 'Ah, there he is, the darling,' she yelled, 'there's that little boy again, only this time he's got a moustache.'

Poor Ernie was completely thrown off balance and even lost his moustache! We quickly wound up the sketch. We were a very happy company whatever our problems. I had with me Gerry Hoey and his band, comedian Joe King and Marie Lloyd's sisters, Alice and Rosie.

During the same year, I was one of the stars of a radio show called *Saturday Social*, which was built around that well-known music-hall comedian, Billy Russell, in his working-man character. He was supposed to be running a working men's club and it was his idea that he should wear his usual costume—corduroys with a strap around each knee, a rough jacket, spotted muffler and battered old trilby, so that we could really capture the atmosphere before the mike. Jeanne de Casalis was cast as the barmaid and Phyllis Robins and myself were there to entertain the club members. Unfortunately, this was one of those shows which failed to click and lasted for about eight weeks before being taken off.

I was very fond of Billy; he was a grand old trouper who had spent all his days knocking around the music halls. No artist knew more about rough theatres and even rougher theatrical digs than Billy. He made his first stage appearance at the age of seven. After the war, he ran into a lean period—as we all do from time to time—and came to see me when we were rehearsing one of the early Dixon programmes. I tried very hard to find a part for him in one of the weekly shows, but regrettably, there was nothing suitable for his particular—and considerable—talent. I was as disappointed as old Bill, but as events turned out he had no need to worry. He was snapped up by I.T.V. and appeared in countless plays, thus starting a new career as a straight actor when he was well over seventy.

Later he was given parts in a number of B.B.C plays and made quite a hit in several West End productions. At seventy-seven he was starring in the B.B.C.'s *Comedy Playhouse.*

In our business when you're down you are really on the floor and when you're up everything turns into gold—that's how it always seems to work out—and true to this pattern, just as Billy was snowed under with parts, we wanted him twice for the Dixon series. He was able to accept the work and having him around was really great.

Bill always had a gag on the tip of his tongue and was very clever at up-dating chestnuts. Everyone knows the old one, 'Who was that lady I saw you with last night?'—'That was no lady, that was my wife!'

His version to fit the unisex age was, 'Who was that lady I saw you with last night?'—'That was no lady, that was my nephew, I keep trying to tell him.'

Just before he returned to this country from Australia, where he did a mammoth tour in about 1955–6, a London newspaper reported that he had died and printed an obituary notice. Bill was highly amused. 'It's not the first time,' he said. 'I've been killed off on several occasions but I always pop up again.' In fact, he died in 1971.

The year 1942 was a melancholy one for me because my mother died in March of that year. I have already said what a marvellous woman she was to all of us, but I should add she was also a keen critic of Elsie, Doris and myself. When we were performing in town, she would often slip quietly into the theatre without us knowing and catch our acts. She was as equally ready with criticism as she was with praise but she was also very proud of her 'kids'.

Mother used to boast, 'My John, with his blue pencil gag, has stopped the whole nation from swearing.' I think she really believed that—bless her! But if she had been alive today, oh dear. . .!

Only a few days after her death, I was convicted of driving without due care and attention at Richmond, Surrey, and was fined ten pounds and had my licence suspended for a month. I hit a cyclist I failed to see late at night in the black-out. It was a bit ironic because when I left my car to assist the cyclist, I tripped and fell on my face. Fortunately, the cyclist was not seriously injured. I didn't care a damn about my facial bruises but I did care about my battered pride. I was furious with myself when I recalled all the years I had been driving without blemish.

1942 was an eventful year, too, because it marked my entry into the film business. I appeared—as myself—in a picture alled *The Dummy Talks*.

CHAPTER 5

Royal Appearance

ANY PERSON who embarks upon a theatrical career has to be something of an extrovert or even an exhibitionist and the profession is unique because it combines three things: an outlet for the individual artiste's talents and exhibitionism and, given good fortune, pleasure for the artiste's audience, plus the added bonus of job satisfaction.

Often the performer is only as good as his audience encourages him to be. I quickly learned that when I first walked on to the stage and was picked up by the spotlight. The audience's initial reception, that is the round of applause usually accorded to any performer, signifies very little. Usually it is restrained because you know that the people whose faces are only blobs in the black-out beyond the footlights are already asking themselves, 'What is he going to do for us?' The response to the first joke is also not very indicative of the way the show will go because the audience is still in a state of anticipation which they are not certain will be fulfilled.

During my first two minutes on any large stage, I feel the most lonely and friendless person in the world. It is only when the audience follow a prolonged laugh with generous applause that I feel assured that they are my friends. Immediately such an intimacy is established, I relax and my performance becomes better and better. To overcome that lukewarm spell of audience reaction, before a television comedy and music spot actually reaches the screen, the studio audience is taken through a 'warm-up' period. By the time the show appears in your living room, the audience's enthusiasm has matured and is instantly communicated to the viewers. But despite the hazards of performing live, like most older artists, I prefer it, because I respond swiftly to the friendliness of the public.

It may seem strange to readers that I should have felt the same way even when broadcasting. To me, the microphone was not just an inanimate object. When I addressed it, I was talking to people in their armchairs at home and to me they were identifiable. My emotions are also activated by other people around me—especially with a show like *Garrison Theatre* when we were touring and pooling personal problems. We were taking part daily in what I might term group therapy and in such a personal environment, when everyone voices his or her troubles, one soon discovers a talent for putting the difficulties of life in their true perspective.

As soon as I walked on to the set of my first film, *The Dummy Talks*, I sensed a complete absence of show business atmosphere and it seemed as if I had entered a factory. Indeed, I was to discover during my career in films that the making of pictures was not all that far removed from the manufacture of motor cars. There were components to be made and then assembled, as in industry, and even in the bigger and more important films there was so much dispersal that one was able to meet only those fellow players directly involved with you in a particular scene. The film was made in sections and shot at different times and in different sets.

The first film in 1942 was of necessity a low budget picture. Money and equipment were terribly short and it was extremely difficult for distributors to feed the cinema with any British-made productions. The story of *The Dummy Talks* was about the murder of a ventriloquist during a music-hall show. The film was really a vehicle which enabled the director, Oswald

Mitchell, to introduce a cast of variety top-liners of the day. He was anxious for me to cash in on the success of *Garrison Theatre* and do the 'My bruvver Sid' letters but I wasn't keen on the idea because I felt this particular act was rapidly becoming old hat. I did, however, do some of the stuff I trotted out in *Garrison Theatre* during the 'variety show' in which the ventriloquist was killed.

Beryl Orde and Ivy Benson and her All Ladies Band also had spots in the film, and Claude Hulbert—who made me fall about laughing—played the part of a dithering special constable.

It was quite a pleasant little picture for its period, but as with many other old movies, its lack of sophistication in this day and age would probably destroy its appeal.

After the second day's shooting, somebody asked me if I intended seeing the rushes—film of the previous day's work. I entered a little darkened studio and sat next to Oswald Mitchell. The silence was broken by the whirring of the projector—and there I was on the screen!

I shall never forget that first time of seeing myself in a movie. Nowadays, when many people record their family holidays with cine cameras, it would mean little. But I remember remarking, rather inanely, 'That's not me!'

As soon as I heard my voice I knew just how nervous I had been during the shooting because I was rushing my words and the pitch of my voice was slightly raised. I have always been a severe critic of my own work and realising what was wrong, I fought my tension the following day so that my whole performance was much more controlled.

The following year, 1943, I teamed up with Ivy Benson and her band in a new radio series created for me called *Jack's Dive*, which was supposed to be a roadhouse. I was the proprietor of the establishment and Claude Allister took the part of the manager. I wonder how many people remember Claude, who had returned from Hollywood where he had been for six years making a name for himself as the typical English dude. Probably some picturegoers of the thirties will recall him as Algie in the

Bulldog Drummond movies. Strangely, although he had done so much work in Hollywood, he had never before appeared in radio in this country. An actress who has raised many a laugh in all types of entertainment was our guest star on the first broadcast—Joyce Grenfell.

I was extremely busy throughout the war years, doing variety, appearing at troop concerts and charity shows, and in 1944 I took the male lead in a musical comedy called *Full Swing*, which had run for eighteen months at the Palace Theatre, London, and had been specially written for Jack Hulbert and Cicely Courtneidge.

Tom Arnold produced the show on tour. We opened at Nottingham and went on to Birmingham and Edinburgh. I took over Jack's role and Marie Marion played Cicely's part. It was my first and only appearance in a musical comedy and I know I didn't impress myself—or other people for that matter.

My appearance before the Royal Family was another first-time event for me during the war. The occasion was Princess Elizabeth's sixteenth birthday in April, 1942, when she made what I suppose one would describe as her first official entry into public life by reviewing a special birthday parade of seven hundred officers and men of the Grenadier Guards. Afterwards, Princess Elizabeth gave a party for the guards at Windsor Castle, and I was one of the artistes chosen to entertain the Royal family and their guests. Everything about the castle is rather vast and could have been faintly intimidating for people like me, but the atmosphere was as friendly and warm as that I had encountered so often before in West End cabaret, and I thoroughly enjoyed myself. I was in excellent company. The Forces' Sweetheart, Vera Lynn, was there with Nan Kenway and Douglas Young, Max Geldray, the harmonica wizard, plus Tommy Handley and the *ITMA* cast.

Everything, including my own act, ticked like a well-lubricated machine. King George VI, Queen Elizabeth and the Princesses Elizabeth and Margaret were there, and at the end of my act I asked them to join in a song called 'Oysters and

Clams'. They really had a go—very ably backed by no less than seven hundred guardsmen and officers.

After the show we were entertained to tea and presented to the Royal Family. The King and Queen walked down the long line of artistes standing before the enormous fireplace in the great hall. The two princesses followed their parents and conversation flowed from one to another of us.

One particular aspect of this evening impressed itself upon me and will for ever remain in my memory. King George VI's unfortunate speech impediment—in the form of a slight and, I often thought, rather appealing stammer—was well known to the British public. He had worked tremendously hard to try and overcome it and had practically won the fight. But occasionally his nervous affliction overcame him.

Several times during our presentation, he became a little tongue-tied. When this happened, almost as if she was being cued, the Queen unobtrusively and absolutely naturally took up the conversation for just as many seconds as it took the King to recover and resume talking. It was difficult to look upon them as royalty. They impressed me as a very normal husband and wife, devoted to each other and able to communicate with each other in a way that is only found between two people very much in love and whose lives have been welded into one.

I have met the present Queen several times. Prior to her coronation she visited Ealing Studios while I was filming there and also the Television Centre, where she told me that she thought *Dixon of Dock Green* had become part of the British way of life.

From 1942 onwards, I was often in the company of that great comedian, Sid Field. We used to meet for a drink at the 'Trocadero' at lunchtime when we were both in town.

I had the greatest admiration for him and I don't mind admitting that I shed some tears when I learned of his death while I was in France in 1950. He was a wonderful character, a very lovable man and a brilliant artist. He was sufficiently clever to have the crowds literally rolling in the aisles without having to resort to the blue material which spills out from radio and the television screen today. When he first rang the bell in the West End, he received a letter from the great 'Cocky' (C. B. Cochran) which read, 'It's years since I laughed so much . . . I do hope you will never be persuaded to forget that you were a clean comedian when you came to London. . . .' Sid never did forget. He believed that if a man couldn't win over an audience with untainted wit he had no right to call himself a comedian. He wasn't a prude by any standards but he considered that risqué stories should be told in private when one could choose one's audience and not in public where offence could easily be given and taken.

It is sad to reflect that while he topped bills in the provinces he was unknown in London until he was almost thirty-nine and that he enjoyed less than seven years of success before he died of a heart attack.

In March, 1943, George Black put on a show at the Prince of Wales Theatre called *Strike a New Note*. There were no stars in it in the accepted sense when the show opened. Each artiste was billed in alphabetical order. But within three weeks all advertising matter had been amended to make it clear that Sid—in his very first London appearance—was the king pin of the show. He really did fulfil every performer's dream of being an overnight West End success, yet he was only putting over comedy scenes that had long been familiar in provincial music halls.

But all his material was delightfully new to London audiences and they adored it. He made his entry as the famous spiv character, 'Slasher Green', wearing a vivid emerald bow-tie and near ground-length overcoat with enormous padded shoulders —an act I have seen so often that I could practically do it myself.

I have yet to hear laughter as hearty as I did when Sid was on the stage. He was out of this world, especially in the famous golfing and snooker sketches with Jerry Desmonde who played the patient instructor to Sid's uncomprehending pupil.

I never ceased to be astounded how so many comedians—

and Sid was no exception—managed to become kings of laughter in view of their underprivileged childhood. Born and reared in poverty, their very survival was a miracle. Sid really had a tough time as a kid and was only a child when he first appeared on the stage in his native Birmingham. I remember him telling me that his twenty-first birthday cake was three penn'orth of stale buns eaten in a seedy provincial boarding house and that he was so hard up at one time that he seriously thought of chucking the stage and joining the Merchant Navy. But, happily, that whole scene changed with his West End debut. *Strike a New Note* ran for months and was followed by *Strike it Again* and then *Piccadilly Hayride*. There were films too, and Sid clearly showed that he was more than just a stand-up comic when he took the lead in *Harvey*, the straight play about an imaginary rabbit who is the constant companion of a cheerful alcoholic. It had a highly successful West End run with a cast which included that fine character actress, Athene Seyler.

Everything was going his way. From his humble little semi-detached in Birmingham he moved to a lovely house at Roehampton and, only a year before he died, bought an even more palatial place in Parkside, Wimbledon. His grim childhood made him warmly appreciative of his security and of human bonds. He was a real family man and the greatest pleasure he derived from his success was the chance to provide some of the luxuries of life for his wife, Connie, and three children. He was still playing the lead in *Harvey* when he died so suddenly and tragically, leaving only a few thousand pounds after payment of income tax, surtax and death duties.

I can assert without fear of contradiction that Sid's partner, Jerry Desmonde, was one of the best feeds in the business. For some time he and his wife, Peggy, were a very successful song-and-dance act, but undoubtedly Jerry's real talent was in playing a straight man to comedians. To watch him and Sid together was to witness the act of two truly fantastic professionals. Their timing is only rivalled today by Eric Morecambe and Ernie Wise.

After Sid's death, Jerry disappeared from show business until he reappeared with Norman Wisdom and later Bob Hope. He became well-known to television viewers in the 1950s as a member of the *What's My Line* panel and as compere of another popular television panel game, *The 64,000 Question* (not dollars as so many people think).

In 1957, Associated Television ended his contract and nothing seemed to go right for him from that moment. He appeared in one or two films and in the West End stage version of *Doctor at Sea*, but this closed after only three weeks. Employment in the movie industry is wildly uncertain and fitful for all but international stars. For the more modest player the bread and butter parts so essential to survival are few and far between.

In December, 1966, Jerry's wife died and I think this was the final blow, although when he visited Mollie and me at our home early in the following year, he appeared to be bright and cheerful. Unfortunately, that was only poor old Jerry putting on an act. He took his own life only a few days after seeing us and was found by his son, Gerald, in the flat they shared in St. John's Wood. He had taken a fatal combination of alcohol and sleeping tablets and had left a note declaring his intention. It was a sorrowful parting from friends who remembered happier occasions when Jerry took pleasure in his professional tasks and his high spirits brightened the days for many others.

Jimmy Edwards is another of my great chums in show business. As a top comic, he can be likened in theatrical stature to Sid Field, although his technique is vastly different. His moustache, of course, is his trade mark, and if Jimmy shaved off those whiskers he just wouldn't be the same man. Such enormous moustaches were very popular among flying officers during the last war and Jim formed the Handlebar Club to perpetuate the custom after the war was over and encourage new members.

I doubt if many readers will know that Jim temporarily lost his moustache when the aeroplane he was piloting was attacked and shot down. Jim's moustache went up in flames, his face was badly burned and he was officially reported missing. He was later awarded the D.F.C. for his part in the shoot-up in which three of his comrades died. Typically, if anyone refers to his 'gong', Jim says that he was the only man in the R.A.F. to win the D.F.C. for losing a moustache!

Jim's heart matches his girth and he is an extremely kindly man. He began his career in Cambridge with the Footlights Club but his first professional engagement was among the girls at the famous Windmill Theatre. As is widely known, he never put a foot wrong afterwards. Not his least notable appearances were in the radio shows *Take it from Here*, with Dick Bentley and Joy Nichols, which ran for eleven years, and *Does the Team Think?* which, I believe, was largely devised by him.

I suppose it is inevitable that when one becomes fairly well known in show business, one attracts the mothers of children who are convinced that they have a son or daughter who is a genius. Two mothers who approached me did, in fact, have offspring who, if not world-beaters, were certainly endowed with tremendous talent. One was the late Tony Hancock and the other gorgeous Julie Andrews.

My mother was staying at a Bournemouth hotel with Mollie one year when the proprietress asked mother if Jack Warner was her son. When mother confirmed the relationship, the hotel owner confided that she had a son who was desperately keen to get into show business and she wondered if I might be able to help. Mother agreed to talk to me and when I eventually saw Tony perform, I knew at once that he had a great future before him. He was truly Chaplinesque in the way that he could make pathos and humour come together. I arranged one or two introductions, and eventually he was given a chance by the very man who had done so much for me, Leslie Bridgemont, the B.B.C. producer.

I cannot forget a letter Tony wrote to Mollie in those early days when he was struggling for recognition. It was almost entirely devoted to self-criticism, and written in a mood of desperate melancholia. As soon as we could, we went to see his act and I offered all the encouragement I could muster, but just how do you convince a very funny man that he is a great comic when he is convinced that he isn't?

Leslie had visited Bournemouth for a broadcast early in the war and an audition convinced him that Tony possessed enormous talent. Within weeks his voice, which was to become as familiar as any in the land, was heard for the first time on a Forces' show from Bristol. In 1942, when he joined the R.A.F., Tony became a member of Ralph Reader's *Gang Show* and this gave him the opportunity of acquiring much needed experience in reasonable comfort—as compared with battling as an unknown against music-hall audiences in small provincial theatres. After demobilisation, Tony did reasonably well in summer shows and pantomime and was, in fact, going through what I call the apprenticeship and improvers' bit of the business. But all this came terribly hard to him because he was impatient with himself. He was convinced that he was not climbing fast enough and he was the only person to blame.

Eventually, as with most artists with genuine talent, his break came. He fought for his laughs, as did Jimmy Edwards, at the Windmill Theatre, where he had to be excruciatingly funny to command the attention of a male audience who tended to be seduced by the titillating presence of a bevy of statuesque nudes. Tony triumphed against this tough opposition and his success won him a place in radio and television. He joined the cast of *Educating Archie* with ventriloquist, Peter Brough. The show eventually toured the variety theatres. Tony appeared with Jimmy in *London Laughs* and then starred at *The Talk of the Town*. Not long afterwards he began to make his name in his own radio show, *Hancock's Half-Hour*.

Although his popularity spread with the rapidity of a bush fire, it is almost unbelievable that he should have continued to fret and worry. But he did!

We used to rehearse the *Dixon of Dock Green* episodes at the Sulgrave Boys' Club, Goldhawk Road, Shepherds Bush, at the same time that Tony was busy with his programme in another part of the building and I tried my damnedest to banish his frequent moods of gloom. But I met with little success.

I said to him one day, 'Look, Tony, everything you have done up to now has been right. I see no reason why you should want to change the format of your programme. You get your changes with the different people you introduce on the show but ultimately you are the one who matters. You are the king-pin of *Hancock's Half-Hour* and you have nothing to worry about. Your appearance, the intonation of your voice and the wonderful throwaway technique are all things that have not been done that way before and the reason why you are so admired. Why should you worry?'

'I don't know,' he sadly replied. 'I suppose I'm just made like that.'

He continued to be restless and began talking about going solo. Now, I knew how much courage it took to take that kind of step. I was compelled to do it early in my career and it had caused me plenty of anxiety. For Tony to consider cutting himself off from Sid James, as he later did, could only result in professional suicide.

If Sid had been moulded in clay as Tony's foil he couldn't have fitted the part better, and backed by the wonderful scripts provided by Ray Galton and Alan Simpson I could never see them toppling off the top rung of the show business ladder, but nevertheless, he made the decision.

It became more difficult to understand when one reflected upon the struggle he had had to reach the peak. He was born in the Midlands—it is strange how many first-class comedians have come from these grey areas—and moved to Bournemouth as a small boy when his parents took over the hotel. Tony certainly became stage-struck at an early age. His father died when he was still at school and as soon as he was old enough, he tried his hand at a number of menial jobs as stop-gaps until he could somehow get into show business. He worked in a tailor's shop for a brief time and later became odd-job man at the Pembroke Hotel, Bournemouth.

After parting from Sid James, Galton and Simpson, he made a couple of films, did some work for I.T.V. and achieved some success in cabaret and variety, but nothing seemed to click like *Hancock's Half-Hour*. Every time he made a solo appearance, poor Tony's stomach knotted up in the way it did in the first early days of his career. He suffered agonies.

In the series with Sid, he had created a character the public had taken to their hearts, and he found they were not prepared to accept a substitute they considered inferior. It was Laurel without Hardy and Morecambe without Wise. People began asking what every artist dreads to hear of himself, 'What's happened to Tony Hancock these days?'

It is ironic that his death in Australia in the summer of 1968 brought him more publicity than he had enjoyed for several years. He had plummeted in the popularity chart, so to speak, in Britain and had accepted an offer from Down-Under to appear in a comedy series for television. The plan was for him to star in an indefinite number of half-hour shows in colour, playing a snooty but dejected English migrant on the loose in Sydney. The series was designed for world-wide distribution and could have pulled Tony right up to the top again.

Many people talked about his drinking problem and although I would not suggest that it did not exist, I think it should be put in its proper perspective. He wasn't just a gifted performer who drank away success merely for the sake of self-indulgence, but a great artiste who, in the throes of an acute psychological problem, turned to booze for solace. In fact, before his tragic death, he had been on the wagon for two months—having had treatment in a private Sydney hospital. Three episodes of the new series had been completed and Australian television pundits acclaimed them as being as riotous as anything he had ever done before.

It was on June 25th that he was found dead in his flat in the

Sydney suburb of Bellevue. Beside his body was an empty vodka bottle and a bottle which had contained two hundred sleeping pills. His hand held the pen he had used to write two notes—one included a message of love to his mother—and he had made it clear that he intended to take his life. He was only forty-four years of age.

So much was written about him at the time of the tragedy and afterwards, when practically everyone who had known him rushed into print with their personal, and often conflicting, views on the tragedy of his life and death, that it seems to me no useful purpose can be served by further theorising on the situation. He was a perfectionist, a nervous worrier, often emotionally and sometimes physically sick, and his private life was complicated. His first wife, Cicely, the daughter of an eminent surgeon, divorced him after fifteen years of marriage and a few days before his suicide he learned that his second wife, Freddie Ross, with whom he lived for only seven months, had been granted a decree nisi in London on the grounds of cruelty and adultery. It has been suggested that his second divorce was the final blow to him, but a number of his friends believed that he had never ceased to love Cicely and hoped to re-marry her. She survived him by only six months when she was fatally injured by a fall at her home in South Godstone, Surrey.

Lingfield, where Tony and Cicely lived together when they were married, was the scene of happy but tempestuous days. They liked to go out for a drink and their favourite pubs were 'The Star' at Lingfield, kept by the late Archie Gibbs and his wife, Olive, and 'The Railway Hotel', at South Godstone, whose tenants were Mr. and Mrs. Jack Doubtfire. Tony and Cicely never sought the companionship of the locals. Often Tony, after exchanging only a few words with the landlord, would find some corner near the bar, holding a desultory conversation with his wife. He always appeared worried and would sit hunched over his glass 'looking like a man who had all the cares of the world on his shoulders'.

It is perhaps significant that after they parted and Tony had left the Lingfield family home, Cicely still followed the routine they had shared for several years.

When she went to live alone at her South Godstone cottage, she appeared daily at 'The Railway Hotel'. She was never taciturn and often exchanged greetings with her host. But then she would sit on a bar stool sipping vodka, a lone and melancholy figure with nothing but her memories for companionship.

The Sydney Coroner, Mr. J. J. Loomes, seemed to arrive at the heart of the matter when he said of Tony at the conclusion of the inquest, 'One can only admire his fortitude in carrying out his work and giving pleasure and enjoyment to people when he was beset with problems in his own private life. It is true these problems finally overcame him. Suicide is not a disease, a crime or a sin, but a symptom of many different problems, ranging from chronic mental illness to an impulsive solution, or occasionally a more planned solution, to a crisis in an individual's life. . . .'

Nobody really knew and nobody can ever know what was in Tony's mind or heart when he decided to write 'finis' to a life that could have been so rich, so full and so satisfying. The only thing we can be sure of is that we are all the poorer for his passing.

Fortunately, the story of Julie Andrews is a happier one. She was introduced to me when I was doing a cabaret act at the Connaught Rooms in London in April, 1947, and on the same bill as a talented husband and wife team.

When the show ended, the wife approached me and said, 'You know, Mr. Warner, I have a litte girl who sings. . . .'

Having heard this opening gambit a hundred times before, I did my best to show interest and said, 'Well that's great. What kind of song does she sing?'

'Anything—absolutely anything,' replied the mother. 'Opera, popular songs, you name it. Could you spare a little time to hear her?'

I won't pretend I was all that keen, but the family didn't live too far from London—at Walton-on-Thames—so I agreed to visit them within a few days.

The little girl walked into the room—serene, extremely polite and certainly not aggresively confident. I waited . . . her mother played a few chords at the piano and the child began to sing. To say that I was astonished is putting it very mildly. In all my travels, I had heard only one voice comparable for its extraordinary range and purity—that of Gracie Fields.

As I listened to this remarkable child, my mind raced back to the first time I listened to Gracie. It was during a music-hall show at the old Alhambra one night soon after the end of World War I, long before I had even given a thought to becoming a professional entertainer. Gracie came on to the stage, wearing a gym slip, tam-o-shanter and with her hair in plaits, and as she started to sing I turned to my brother and whispered, 'That girl is going right to the top.'

I felt exactly the same as I listened to Julie. Her voice, even at that age, was really much better than Gracie's. I asked her mother how long she had been singing in this way—her range would have been remarkable if she had been adult—and she said from very early childnood.

It so happened that I was then arranging a Sunday concert for the British Legion and Julie's mother was only too delighted to agree to her young daughter appearing on the bill.

Julie was Barbara's daughter by her first marriage and her name had been changed when her mother married Ted Andrews after her divorce. The little girl had been as stage-struck as Tony Hancock and had first caught the bug when she appeared in a dancing-school concert at Walton-on-Thames at the age of two! But it wasn't until she sang 'Strawberry Fair' in an air-raid shelter during a heavy bombing raid that Barbara and Ted realised the amazing quality of her voice. Several neighbours had fled to the shelter that night and when those high, pure notes came flowing effortlessly from Julie the little company, huddled together, forgot the menace of the bombs and the shattering noise of anti-aircraft fire. They were too enthralled to be frightened.

Barbara told me that she and Ted had felt some concern at

first about encouraging the development of a big voice in so small a girl. They thought it might prove injurious to the vocal chords but a throat specialist had assured them that if her training was properly controlled, no damage would be done. They did the wise thing and sent Julie to a well-known concert singer who taught voice production.

She absolutely stopped the show when she appeared at the Legion concert. Later she was auditioned by Val Parnell and began her professional career in the revue, *Starlight Roof* at the London Hippodrome when she was twelve years old. Since then, I need hardly say, she has never looked back nor is ever likely to!

There was another artiste on the *Starlight Roof* bill who I like to think I gently nudged along the road to show business success. It was Michael Bentine, whose father was a great friend of mine.

Soon after the war, I met Adam Bentine and he said to me, 'My son, Michael, is coming out of the Royal Air Force soon and he has what I think is a very funny act. I wonder if you could give him a helping hand in the business?'

He introduced me to his son and he was certainly unlike any other comedian I had ever seen or heard. With his mop of dark hair and luxuriant beard (this was long before beards became fashionable again) he looked as unlikely a comic as the Archbishop of Canterbury. Before joining the R.A.F. he had been a Shakespearean actor and had appeared in the open-air presentations in Regent's Park and possessed a fine resonant voice. But I soon discovered that beneath his talent as a straight actor, he had a peculiar brand of crazy humour that would make people either love or hate him. I found him very, very funny and wasted no time in introducing him to Val Parnell.

Michael made his debut in *Starlight Roof* with an original and inspired piece of fooling with the back of a bentwood chair in which he illustrated the innumerable uses to which it could be put. Within a few weeks we were reading about the discovery of a brilliant new comedian. Less than a year later, he was the hit of *Folies Bergère* at the London Hippodrome—which led to his appearance in the 1949 Royal Command Variety show. I sometimes wondered if it would have been wiser to have abandoned my stage career and earned my living as an agent!

Michael told me how his strange chair-back act was born. He was rehearsing Shakespeare for an impending audition when he fell across a chair and broke it—and that gave him the idea of using the chair-back in a comic context. That fragment of furniture, plus the sink plunger he used, became almost human in his hands.

He is a truly remarkable man of many talents. Educated at Eton, he speaks five or six languages, is a brilliant mathematician, an astronomer, Egyptologist, skilled archer and a crack shot. He also has an extraordinary amount of culinary ability and loves being let loose in the kitchen. Yet until he was eighteen, he had such a dismaying stammer that he scarcely spoke to anyone outside his own family.

He told me of an occasion when one day he was feeling hungry and walked into a shop and asked, 'May I have a fish cake?' He swears that he lived off this dish for ages because that was the only sentence he could fluently utter in a shop. Later he went to a speech therapist who solved his problem for him. He is not only an extremely clever writer but invents the gadgets he uses on stage. His show, *It's a Square World*, was one of the most successful of all T.V. series, so much so that hundreds of viewers protested to the B.B.C. when a televised international football match exceeded its scheduled time by half an hour and caused the cancellation of Michael's show that evening.

His father, Adam, is also a remarkable man and my first encounter with him was bizarre to say the least. I was doing a variety show in Bristol in the autumn of 1942 when I sprained my ankle walking across the stage in the dark. I couldn't get a taxi and had to hobble painfully back to my hotel. Adelaide Hall, who was sharing the bill with me, was staying at the same hotel and when she saw me limp in she said that she knew somebody who could help me. She and her husband assisted me to my room and then Adelaide picked up the telephone, asked for a number, and when the connection was made spoke into the telephone thus: 'Mr. Warner is here and he would like to have a word with you.'

I had no idea to whom I was speaking but a man's voice on the other end said, 'You've got something wrong with your foot.' As I had not yet said a word and Adelaide had not mentioned what was wrong with me, I was really taken aback. Then the voice told me not to worry. 'But I am worried,' I protested. 'I've got a *Workers' Playtime* broadcast to do tomorrow as well as a couple of shows at the Empire.'

I was assured that my ankle would be all right by the following day. 'Go to bed and forget about it. Sleep if you can. If anything happens between three and five o'clock in the morning, just don't take any notice,' was the advice I received.

Adelaide then told me I had been speaking to a Mr. Adam Bentine. 'He is a very extraordinary man,' she confided. I was only too pleased to crawl into bed and rest my ankle but I had grave doubts about those telephone assurances I had received.

I dozed first and then slept afterwards, but awoke after about an hour or so and struggled out of bed. My ankle promptly folded beneath me. I got back into bed with some difficulty, more than ever convinced that only a miracle would enable me to fulfil my engagements the next day. Eventually I managed to fall asleep until I was awakened by the most weird sensation. It felt as though someone had grabbed my injured ankle and was twisting and turning it. In my dazed state, I suddenly remembered the telephone conversation. I looked at my watch. It was 3.45 a.m.—and Adam Bentine had told me to take no notice if something occurred between three and five in the morning!

I knew nothing more until the chambermaid arrived with morning tea. As soon as she departed, I jumped out of bed to test my ankle. It was perfectly O.K. The pain had vanished and there was no suggestion of weakness. The sprain had been cured during the night. I couldn't think of anyone who would listen to this story and believe it, but it happened exactly as I have described.

Shortly afterwards, I met the owner of the voice. He could not explain what had happened—nor would he say why many of the predictions he subsequently made about my future came true.

Michael's father was a Peruvian, but although he came to Britain at the age of thirteen he never adopted British nationality. I've often wondered whether there is anything in the belief that the seventh son of a seventh son does possess strange powers, because that was what Adam was. His father was Don Antonion Bentine, Vice-President of the Peruvian Republic.

Adam was educated in England and became an aeronautic engineer, and a founder member of the Aeronautical Inspection Department in 1941. He was co-designer of a seaplane and inventor of various patents connected with aeroplane safety devices. All his patents were made over to the nation, among them the strain gauge still used in rigging vintage aircraft. He designed various aircraft and testing equipment and envisaged many of the principles still used in aircraft design. In 1919 he returned to Peru to build up the Peruvian Air Force but because of political changes he returned to this country four years later.

In 1924 Adam retired and began to study certain phenomena until his death in 1963. He was a true scientist, investigating phenomena for their own sake, and he was absolutely fearless.

Inevitably he had to endure ridicule and some social ostracism, but he always knew the price he would have to pay for expounding his ideas and theories and expected nothing in return.

I became very friendly with him after that odd incident in Bristol and he often attended my shows.

For about the last twelve months of the war, and immediately after its end, I did a variety act with a big Centurion tank specially constructed for me. It wasn't terribly successful, although I got a few laughs when I was pushing it around the stage. But I had to face the fact that people were then getting a bit fed up with anything to do with the army. They were anxious to forget the horrors of war and get on with the reconstruction of their lives in peacetime.

Adam came backstage to see me one night after the show and at once said, 'You're worried about something.'

'Oh, I'm not really,' I said.

He insisted that although it was not apparent to the audience, my concern was obvious to him and I admitted that I did have something of a problem on my mind. I told him I had been asked to go to Germany to entertain the troops, but that there were one or two other things to be considered and I didn't know what to do for the best. He asked me to pass him a ring I was wearing and he held it in his hands for a little time without saying anything.

Then he suddenly told me, 'You are going to Germany but it will be to do something you have never done before. You are going to work for a firm for which you have not worked before and it will all happen in a few weeks' time.'

I was left wondering. . . .

CHAPTER 6

On Location in Germany

UNTIL MOLLIE heard my future with *Garrison Theatre* predicted by a clairvoyant I had never paid any attention to so-called fortune-telling. But the inexplicable incident over my ankle injury had heightened my interest in the subject and made me wonder even more whether there were really some strange phenomena at work that controlled our destiny. However, when several weeks had gone by without anything occurring to confirm the prediction of Adam Bentine, I became both curious and perhaps sceptical. I could not, though, entirely dismiss the matter from my mind and eventually, overcome by eagerness, I telephoned him and reminded him that I was still waiting for something to happen.

Very nonchalantly and confidently Adam assured me, 'It will . . .'

Not many weeks later I received a letter from Sir Michael Balcon, of Ealing Studios, offering me a part in a film about British prisoners-of-war and advising me that if I accepted, I would be expected to travel to Germany on location within ten days.

Sir Michael sent me the script—and I liked it. When filming

had been completed and I returned to England, Adam told me that I was commencing another phase of my life. He predicted that the film would receive good notices but that it would be the fourth film I made which would be my 'real beginning'. He was absolutely right. The fourth film was called *Holiday Camp* and was made up of a series of episodes, each featuring at least one star and in which Kathleen Harrison and myself were teamed in one small sequence as Mr. and Mrs. Huggett. For some reason, this episode proved exceptional and led to three more Huggett films, plus nine years of a radio series entitled *Meet The Huggetts.*

The original title of the Ealing film made in Germany was *Lovers' Meeting* which didn't appeal to anyone involved with the film and I was delighted when my suggestion that it should be changed to *The Captive Heart* was adopted. A great number of the public will have seen it—either in the cinema or on television.

The film had what we used to call an all-star cast, but everyone got on well together. There were no clashes of temperament, as sometimes occur on the set, and although the subject was serious and sometimes rather sad, all of us enjoyed working together. It took four months to complete the film. We were all billeted together in a small hotel in Stada for seven or eight weeks which meant that being so confined some differences of opinion in working and leisure time might have been expected.

This very situation caused me some deep thought while we were shooting camp scenes at Morlag prisoner-of-war camp in Westertimke. We were there in August, 1945, and until just a few weeks previously, it had actually been in use by British P.O.W.s. We made the daily twenty-mile journey from Stada to the camp in a Bedford truck.

My part in the film was that of a Cockney corporal and, such was the atmosphere of the camp, that I very soon began to live the part. Spending every day under the same conditions as the thousand prisoners who had been incarcerated there during the war, we really got the feel of what internment meant. A great part of the story was acted out in the camp rooms, with bare wooden floors, straw-filled mattresses on narrow double-decker bunks, and chairs made from Red Cross packing cases. The cameras panned to clothes drying on home-made clothes' racks, old boots on top of the coffin-like lockers, packs of grimy playing cards, cherished letters from home and packets of cigarettes and of course the pin-ups. Each room was identical. In a space measuring twenty-four feet by twelve feet, up to twenty men had spent precious years of their lives, eating, sleeping and trying to combat boredom and frustration. Whether they liked or hated each other they were aware that there could be no relief until the war ended.

No matter how absorbed I became in my job as a make-believe prisoner, I could not help thinking of the fellows who had actually lived—and sometimes died—in the surroundings in which I was working. I confess that at the end of each day I was glad to climb into the truck—oblivious to the discomfort of the ride—and get back to our hotel. There is no surer way to break a man's heart than to take away his liberty and that feeling came through very strongly during my stay at the camp.

The situation probably meant more to me than to some of the others because my brother Bill (Bernard), who had been a pilot in World War I, was taken prisoner after being shot down. The ruling at that time was that any pilot who lost his plane in this way must set fire to it. Tracer bullets melted in the fire gave the appearance of being soft-nosed dum-dum bullets which were as taboo in World War I as was poison gas in the second. Because of their suspicions regarding the purpose of these bullets the Jerries, just for the hell of it, twice took him out into the yard, stuck him up against a wall, rattled their rifle locks and as good as told him, 'If you don't say what we want you to say, you've had it.' He refused to admit what was untrue—that he had used dum-dum bullets—and eventually they ceased threatening him.

During the making of *The Captive Heart* I could understand what poor old Bill had gone through. He was a very quiet type of chap and could put up with a lot, but he hated to be shut up anywhere even for five minutes. To be trapped in a prisoner-of-war camp must have caused him a great deal of distress. He was one of the first of the inmates to try tunnelling his way out but he didn't make it and was forced to remain in the camp for a further eighteen months. He died in 1950 and I often think that his ill-health was rooted in the prisoner-of-war camp all those years ago.

Apart from the absolute authenticity of the setting, much of the feeling of realism about the film came from the fact that one of the scriptwriters, R.N.V.R. Lieutenant Guy Morgan, had actually been a prisoner at Morlag. We were given a lot of help by the War Office and the British Army of the Rhine and five hundred real soldiers—officers and men—who took part in the film. They were mostly from the Middlesex Regiment and the Argyll and Sutherland Highlanders. It was interesting to get among these fellows on location, to join in their parties at the sergeant's mess and officer's mess and to hear at first hand of their war experiences.

During this period, we met a young man named John Worsley, an official war artist, who had been a prisoner at the camp. He showed us big pictures that had been painted on the walls of one of the huts, depicting women either nude or in various stages of undress. Worsley told us that at night the Germans would direct searchlights through the windows to illuminate these pictures—a refined type of torture for the men inside who had not seen a woman in the flesh for up to five years. The Germans employed all kinds of tricks to destroy morale but the prisoners in this instance were too smart for them and spoiled their fun by covering up the naked ladies, leaving their tormentors with nothing to illuminate.

The action of the film started on the first Christmas of the war and it was necessary to have a long shot of the camp under a heavy blanket of snow. But as we were working there in the summer of 1945, the snow had to be manufactured. The Army Fire Service obliged by spraying the whole place with foam, and it really looked authentic. It almost felt like snow as we walked through it and the cameraman prepared for shooting—but then down came the rain and washed it all away.

Another attempt was made the following morning, but no sooner had the foam been sprayed than a hot sun began to dry it and a sudden and powerful wind carried it away.

It was not until the fourth day that weather conditions were absolutely right and in the completed film the snow sequence lasted precisely two minutes. Four days for two minutes' film! I was new to filming then but it opened my eyes to the amount of time and money that can be wasted if one is not lucky with the weather.

The Captive Heart consisted largely of a number of cameos of the principle Morlag characters. Sir Michael Redgrave played a Czech officer who had assumed the identity of a dead British soldier, whose widow was none other than Rachael Kempson, Michael's wife in real life.

Another tale concerned the problems of a blind officer—wonderfully well played by Gordon Jackson, when he was an unknown youngster. Today as Hudson the butler he has helped to make the A.T.V. series *Upstairs Downstairs* an enormous success.

As the Cockney corporal, my mate was Private Evans, played by Mervyn Johns, and we shared what I think was one of the most touching moments of the film. Mervyn's 'wife' had died while he was imprisoned and I had to take him home to London with me when the war came to an end. We are seen jumping off the tailboard of a lorry and then humping our kitbags along the mean little street in which I lived. I knock on the door of my house to be welcomed by my 'wife', played by Gladys Henson, but before I can greet her Mervyn says, 'Hello, Flo, we're back.' I look at her, step closer, touch her hair and then utter the first words I had spoken to her for six years—'It suits you.'

It was only a small scene but it brought home to everybody just what reunions were like for thousands of fighting men who finally came back.

The scene, and the way it was played, did not go unmarked

because I was asked to repeat it in another film in which I appeared. I declined because the circumstances were altogether different and it would have sounded absolutely false.

Some members of the profession seem to think that small parts are hardly worth playing but I've never shared this view. It is not always the stars who are remembered the longest. For example, let me tell you something more about *The Captive Heart*, in which you will recall I played the role of a corporal. In one of the first scenes I am trying to overcome boredom by carving a model boat. It is the winter of 1940, with snow on the ground, and everybody bitterly cold because the old stove in our hut lacks fuel. As I stand there whittling away at a piece of wood I know my companions are looking at me. The boat on which I have been working for weeks is almost finished—but I know what is expected of me. At last I open the door of the stove and fling the boat on the dying embers, and at that moment somebody calls out, 'The Red Cross parcels have arrived.' My fellow prisoners rush out of the hut, leaving me, the sad corporal, alone to watch my lovely boat, on which I have for so long laboured, going up in flames.

The scene was not much more than a fragment of prison psychology but seven or eight years later I happened to be a guest at a film party given by the Rank Organisation. Among those present were Van Johnson, Fred MacMurray, Richard Widmark and several other Americans. I hadn't met any of them previously but I noticed Richard Widmark staring intently at me from the other side of the room. He walked across, hand outstretched, and said, 'You're the guy who burned the boat, aren't you?'

Mervyn Johns was a great character to work with, always faultlessly on cue, as one would expect of a dedicated professional, but he had a funny way of twitching one eyelid very quickly and instead of concentrating on my own lines, I began to watch him until, finally, I could stand it no longer. We were good pals and I broke off and said, 'For goodness sake, Mervyn, stop twitching your eye.' Of course, I spoilt the take and we had to start afresh. Later Mervyn told me that when acting, it is quite impossible to look someone straight in the eye. Whenever it is attempted the eyes will go up and down and from side to side and eventually one becomes cross-eyed. The trick, he told me, is to concentrate the gaze upon the bridge of the other person's nose and then the look can be held steady almost indefinitely.

While we were in Germany I organised a little concert party to entertain the troops working with us on the film. I did the old sketch, 'The Plumber's Mate', that I had done on the music halls and Mervyn obligingly dressed up as a woman to partner me. He was a very successful comedian. Then six of us appeared as A.T.S. girls, using lots of make-up and magnificent false bosoms. We clumped—it is more accurate to say than danced! —around the stage while Michael Redgrave played the piano accompaniment to some silly songs.

Among other well-known actors in the film were Basil Radford, as the senior camp officer who measured his years in captivity by the number of Derbys he had missed; Guy Middleton and Derek Bond, both of whom served as officers in the British Army and were appropriately cast as officers in the film; Karl Stepanek, whose portrayal of a member of the Gestapo was most life-like and Jack Lambert who played the padre.

There was also Sam Kydd, an extremely amiable chap with a great sense of humour. Sam had done a bit af acting before the war but, as a member of the Territorial Army, he was among the first draft to be called up. Five days after landing in France he was captured and spent the rest of the war in prison camps in Poland and Germany. His very first post-war part was as a prisoner-of-war in *The Captive Heart.* I felt that the film must have brought some pretty grim memories back to Sam and this was borne out when he became the 'victim' on Eamonn Andrews' *This Is Your Life* programme and the courageous tale of his escape from a camp was colourfully unfolded.

The war may have taken a chunk out of his career but Sam

has more than made up for lost time. He was Patrick Allen's co-star in *Crane* on television and he did so well with the part of Orlando that he was given his own series under the same title. He was in a Harry Worth series, with Spike Milligan in *Curry and Chips* and I believe his appearances in films and television shows now total something like one hundred and fifty. We have been pleased to welcome him on four occasions in the *Dock Green* series.

Another member of the cast I recall with great affection was the late Jimmy Hanley, invalided out of the Commandos. He turned in a lovely performance as an ex-burglar conscripted as a private. Although only in his twenties at that time, he was already a veteran actor. He once told me that when only a lad he was auditioned for *White Horse Inn* at the Coliseum and was one of many little boys paraded before the German director. At the end of the line-up, the director said, 'No, I want the little boy with the big head.' That was Jimmy.

He suffered a lot of reverses but managed to bounce back. For a time Jimmy was a circus artist and he made more than seventy films. Many people will remember Jimmy's association with an I.T.V. advertising magazine, *Jim's Inn*, which lasted for eight years. When it ceased Jimmy found himself without a job. What did he do? He became the landlord of 'The Plough' at Effingham, Surrey.

No less than three million listeners used to tune into his Sunday radio programme, *Start the Day Right*, and he began a new series called *Out and About* when he was taken ill in September, 1969. He was only fifty-one when he died a year later.

We had been friends for twenty-five years and I was greatly upset by his death. Although he was much younger than me, he had started filming long before I did and I was ever grateful to him for the useful advice he gave me. I was reminded of Jimmy only a short time ago when I was confronted by a very tall young man who asked me if I remembered him. I certainly knew his face, especially when he grinned and said, 'You knew my father's face better.'

It was Jeremy Hanley, Jim's son. Jeremy, my godson, had made a brief appearance as a baby in *Holiday Camp*, the film that proved so significant for me.

During the filming of *The Captive Heart*, I had my first experience of a strike. In one of the last scenes there was a bonfire to celebrate the end of the war. It was staged in the studio and that seriously limited its extent, but with the aid of methylated spirits something fairly realistic was produced.

There were quite a number of people in the scene—some genuine soldiers and airmen as well as crowd extras. I was standing and talking to a well-decorated ex-pilot when we noticed the crowd artistes chatting together. Suddenly they all turned and walked off the set.

'What's the trouble?' asked the perplexed pilot. I didn't know myself until I walked over to the extras. They told me that they were asking for danger money because of the fire!

I returned to the pilot, looked at his medal ribbons and thought of all he had been through and told him. He shook hands with me, turned around and walked straight out of the place. Who could blame him? He had seen more danger than the others were likely to see during the whole of their lives.

Adam Bentine was uncannily correct in his prophecy about my career. When *The Blue Lamp* was first shown in 1949, he said it would have far-reaching effects on my life. He told his son Michael, 'This film will make Jack the most famous policeman in Britain.'

Returning briefly to the question of small parts, I could not believe this prediction would prove correct because the copper I played was killed quite early in the film and anyway, the part was a comparatively minor one. Yet it was *The Blue Lamp* that was to lead me into *Dixon of Dock Green*—and I've been Dixon ever since.

Adam Bentine's death at the age of seventy-seven was a great blow to many people. For years he had suffered from asthma and later from nervous debility and his death followed prolonged Parkinson's disease.

His son is a believer in psychic phenomena and he told me that this had helped him to accept the passing (he never uses the word death) of his eldest son.

This lad, Stuart Bentine, and his friend, Andrew Slade, disappeared after taking off in a private aeroplane from Lasham Airfield in Hampshire on August 28th, 1971. Nine weeks later the wreckage of the aeroplane was found only sixteen miles away in Queen Elizabeth Forest, near Petersfield.

A Department of Trade and Industry investigation failed to reveal conclusively the cause of the crash and at the adjourned inquest on the two young men in January 1972, verdicts of 'accidental death' were returned.

CHAPTER 7

The Huggetts and other Movies

THE RANK ORGANISATION asked me to sign a contract following the completion of *The Captive Heart*, which meant that I would be assured of a regular income whether or not I was filming. A relative newcomer, I signed for seven years, believing that the salary I would receive would indeed provide me with a very substantial financial cushion. After four years, during which I made ten films, it struck me forcibly that the Rank Organisation were getting more than their pound of flesh. The whole system was, as I discovered, extremely inequitable because while I was making ten films, many other players under contract were making far fewer or none at all. I asked for an increase and the figure was stepped up.

I was, of course, extremely happy to be kept busy, but I've never been much of a business man and in retrospect I now see that if I had possessed any real ability as a negotiator, I would have struck a much better bargain.

I made a lot of films with Rank—twenty-seven of them during the first eleven years after the war. Some, of course, were less successful than others but, without being too boastful, I think I can claim to have made a reasonably useful contribution to the industry. In 1950 I topped the *Motion Picture Herald* poll as the British male star who had attracted most money to the box offices. Anna Neagle was the top British woman star that year.

One thing which does please me when I reflect upon those busy years is that with the exception of *Holiday Camp* and the three Huggett pictures—in which I played the part of Joe Huggett—I portrayed a different character every time. I fought hard against being type-cast and I think I won my battle by playing everything from detective inspector to murderer, from Borstal governor to spiv, and from crack cricketer to traitor. I know that everyone now regards me only as a kindly copper—and I have certainly had more than my share of policeman parts—but when I was making films for the cinema, I looked upon it as a challenge to do something different every time.

Soon after the completion of *The Captive Heart* I heard that Michael Balcon was planning a film about a black marketeer, a really villainous type fated to meet a sticky end at the hands of a bunch of kids. I was interested in the role but Micky Balcon was not very keen. 'I don't think it's quite you,' he said. 'This warm Cockney corporal you created in the last film must go on for a little while.'

'But I don't want to perpetuate that image,' I protested. 'If I'm going to continue making pictures, I want to play different people.'

Michael appreciated my point but he didn't think I could look sufficiently sinister. I argued with him until he agreed that I should at least be tested for the part.

I put on a moustache—I had worn one when young to make myself look older and later shaved it off to make myself look younger!—donned a mackintosh with the collar up-turned, tipped my hat at an angle and stuck a cigarette in the corner of my mouth. I then stepped through a doorway in half-light. I got the part!

The title of the film was *Hue and Cry*. It was produced on a budget of around £80,000 and made a great deal more money than many other films which cost twice as much to make. It had tremendous appeal because there were between two hundred and three hundred youngsters in it—some on bicycles and others on tricycles, a popular mode of transport when shops employed errand boys.

The plot concerned a gang of thieves who used a serial story in a boys' paper to exchange coded messages. One of the kids stumbled upon the activities of the gang and their methods and rallied all his pals to track us down.

One of the most exciting scenes in the film was shot in a derelict building near Charing Cross Station—and in 1946 it wasn't difficult to find such a place. It was about ten or twelve storeys high and it was there that I was trapped and chased by the boys. I had to sprint through this depressing ruin with its broken steps and rotten floors until, eventually, one of the lads pushed me through a hole in the floor. I was supposed to fall eight storeys to my death. In fact I fell backwards from the eighth to the seventh floor and into a stretched tarpaulin. The drop was more than enough and not something to be done every day.

The director was Charlie Crichton, who made me perfect an awful laugh. I have worked with him on several occasions and admire the talent which enabled him to create such successes as *The Lavender Hill Mob* and in contrast, *Man in the Sky*, a tense story starring the late Jack Hawkins, and more recently, the highly successful television series, *Black Beauty*.

Alastair Sim took the part of the bumbling author of the boys' serial used by the crooks and brought his quite unique professionalism to the part. I write unique advisedly because many people can impersonate Jimmy Cagney, Jimmy Stewart, Cary Grant, Harold Wilson and Ted Heath, but I've yet to see anyone try to imitate Alastair.

One of the young lads was Harry Fowler, then aged eighteen. He has appeared with me several times in Dixon. Our 'moll' was the girl Harry later married, Joan Dowling—in her first film part—who died in tragic circumstances when only twenty-six.

Joan and Harry met on the set of *Hue and Cry*. He was a former newspaper seller just coming to the front as an actor. She had worked in a soap factory before getting her big opportunity in the role of a Cockney evacuee kid in the stage production of *No Room at the Inn*. Although only about sixteen, Joan made a terrific impact in this and was signed up immediately by Rank.

The pair were inseparable and were married in 1951, six years after their first meeting. They were both successful in their respective careers and were undoubtedly lucky in marriage, but one evening in March, 1954, they went to a party at the 'Jack of Clubs' in Soho to celebrate the Press preview of Harry's latest film, *Conflict of Wings*. Joan appeared to be extremely happy, danced almost throughout the evening and asked the orchestra to play her favourite tunes. They joined Jack Hylton at his table and were delighted when he invited them to the first night of his new show, *Pal Joey*. That date was for the following evening. But it was a date that was not kept. . . .

Joan left the club a little earlier than Harry, who drove some friends home and then, realising that he had not got his door key, decided to stay with the friends rather than disturb his wife.

The following morning, Joan was found gassed in the kitchen of their converted cottage at Notting Hill. It was apparent from the evidence given at the inquest that she had intended to take her life but her reasons remain a mystery.

I was shocked. Joan was my 'daughter' and Harry my 'son' in the radio version of *The Huggetts*. At the time of her death, we had already recorded four programmes in a new Huggett series which were to be broadcast in May that year. They were scrapped and later re-made with Joan's successor.

Harry was so shattered by his young and attractive wife's tragic end that he was written out of the series for a while. He went through a bad patch and I was delighted when he began to recover some of the lost ground. He made a few appearances as a visiting N.C.O. in I.T.V.'s *The Army Game* and was on his way to a rehearsal one day when he noticed a pretty girl arranging a window display in a boutique. He went in and invited her out for coffee, and that was really the beginning of the road back. He had desperately needed someone in his private life who would support him in his difficult struggle.

In November, 1960, he married Kay Palmer, the girl who had given him fresh hope. She was the daughter of a veterinary surgeon from Sturminster Newton, Dorset. By then he had secured the star role of 'Flogger' in *The Army Game*, and has since done well in films and television.

I followed *Hue and Cry* with a film called *Dear Murderer*, in which I made my first screen appearance as a policeman—a detective inspector—and in which Eric Portman starred as a man who plans the perfect murder. The film had a strong cast, which included Hazel Court, Maxwell Reed, Dennis Price and Greta Gynt.

Greta, who was born in Norway and made her first film in Oslo, was one of the glamour girls of the thirties and forties and received so much publicity that it was not often one opened a newspaper without finding some reference to her. She was an extremely gay and light-hearted person and as romantic off screen as on.

I remember that at one of the El Alamein reunions she created something of a sensation by flinging her arms around Field-Marshal Montgomery and giving him a resounding kiss. Then she turned up at one of the Royal Command film shows wearing a silver fox coat over a strapless silver lamé dress, with silver osprey feathers decking her silver-sprayed hair. The visiting American stars were quite put in the shade, which was, of course, the object of the exercise. In those days stars were expected to be eccentric or mildly outrageous and Greta certainly never had any difficulty in dreaming up something that would capture the attention of the public.

After her fourth wedding she gave up acting for a domestic and social life with her husband, leading plastic surgeon

Frederick Moore. But in 1968 she was persuaded to come out of retirement to play Lady Fidget in a new production of Wycherley's *The Country Wife*.

When it came to my next film, I could not help remembering Adam Bentine's prediction that this one, the fourth, was going to mark a turning point in my career. But when I read the script, I entertained very serious doubts about my friend's prognostication. It wasn't that I didn't like my part, but there were others just as good. In a way the scenario was a little like *The Captive Heart* because it was made up of a series of stories set against a common background—in this case a holiday camp which gave the film its title. There was the jilted sailor (the late Jimmy Hanley) who found new romance with a young war widow; Flora Robson, wonderful as a middle-aged spinster; Dennis Price as a bogus squadron leader who turned out to be a sex-killer and the Cockney bus driver and his missus—myself and Kathleen Harrison.

This was the public's introduction to the Huggetts, an ordinary middle-aged couple sampling the high-pressure delights of this type of group holiday for the first time. Pa Huggett became a little flirtatious with the bathing beauties and Ma Huggett tended to nag in a mild way although the couple were devoted to each other. The scene pin-pointed by almost every critic was that in which Ma and Pa Huggett got a bit sentimental when they recalled their honeymoon and he told her that bathing beauties were all right on holiday, 'but for a happy home give me a wife who's plain', to which she replied, 'Oo, thank you, Joe.'

Kathleen and I may have shared a tender moment of connubial warmth and bliss but I can reveal that conditions were hellishly cold! The cameras picked us up on a cliff top by the sea in the midst of brilliant sunshine cooled by a gentle breeze. In fact it was filmed in the old studio at Lime Grove in the winter of 1946–7, with snow on the ground outside and not a breath of warm air to be found anywhere. Kathleen was wearing a light summer frock and I was in cricket shirt and flannels. We were frozen!

The scene made a great impact and of all the characters in the film, the Huggetts created the most appeal, so co-producers Sydney and Muriel Box decided to make a series of Huggett films, commissioning Mabel and Denis Constanduros to write the stories. Sydney's younger sister, Betty, was the producer and Ken Annakin the director.

The structure of the Huggett family underwent some curious changes throughout their film and subsequent radio life. Ma and Pa had a sixteen-year-old son, a war-widowed daughter and a baby grand-daughter when they first appeared in *Holiday Camp*. Hazel Court was the daughter and Peter Hammond—another youngster who achieved success—was the son. As I mentioned earlier, the baby, who was suppposed to be a girl, was Jimmy Hanley's son, Jeremy.

In the following three films, *Here Come the Huggetts*, *Vote for Huggett* and *The Huggetts Abroad*, we were the parents of three lovely daughters. In the first two, the girls were played by Jane Hylton, Susan Shaw and Petula Clark, then a shy girl of fifteen. Jimmy Hanley, who was a sailor in *Holiday Camp*, became an airman who married Jane. By the time we had reached the third film, Jane was no longer available and her part was taken by Dinah Sheridan, who thus found herself playing screen wife to her real life husband, Jimmy Hanley. Peter Hammond, our son in *Holiday Camp*, turned up as Susan's boy friend.

That great actress, Amy Veness, played the part of Grandma Huggett. I first met Diana Dors, then about seventeen, when we were making these films. She appeared in the first as a flighty good-time cousin who managed to create havoc in the family circle. David Tomlinson had a small part in the first film and took one of the leading roles in *Vote for Huggett*.

The films did well and I wasn't exactly surprised when I received a call from the B.B.C. inquiring about the possibility of transferring the Huggetts to radio.

Kathleen and I read some script samples provided by Eddie Maguire and we liked them very much. But by the time *Meet the Huggetts* was first heard on the radio in the middle of 1953 the whole family set-up had changed yet again. This time, Ma and Pa had one daughter and one son—Joan Dowling and Harry Fowler. They had then been married for two years. When Joan died, Vera Day took over her part.

The only members of the family to remain inviolate throughout films and radio were Ma and Pa—otherwise Kathleen and me.

The public seem to accept such changes as part of the cock-eyed business of the entertainment world. They are still greatly intrigued by what goes on at Dock Green even though it is almost twenty-five years since Dixon was killed in *The Blue Lamp*.

All the Huggett films were made at Islington Studios which have now closed. It was originally planned that Jimmy Hanley and I should be flown out to the Sahara for one scene in which we were supposed to be lost in the desert. This would have cost a packet but fortunately proved unnecessary once the technical lads got down to the problem.

These boys behind the scenes rarely receive the recognition they deserve for the sterling work they do. They are able to simulate weather conditions and terrain so exactly and realistically that the filming appears to have been done on location.

In the present case, the technicians cleared the biggest studio at Islington, filled it with sand and with clever lighting provided us with a sun-drenched desert that no moviegoer would have thought was not the genuine article.

Digressing briefly, the only other occasion upon which I entered a studio as lifeless as the Islington one before it became the 'Sahara' was at Shepperton. I walked in with one of the Rank officials. It was empty except for a one-armed bandit covered with a dirty piece of sheeting. I pulled the cover off the machine, rubbed off some dirt, inserted a shilling, pulled the lever and replaced the sheet. I had walked a few yards when I heard a terrific clatter. I'd hit the jackpot and collected six pounds in discoloured shillings!

Performing the Huggetts on the air with other members of the cast was quite different from shooting fragmented sections before cameras. One had to remember that the faintest rustle of the script was magnified a thousand-fold and could easily distract the listeners. Reading from a script is relatively easy but I realised that I never came over nearly as well as I did if I had studied my lines before each broadcast and had had sufficient time to perfect them.

I work even harder on a television script because it is the only way I know to fight the fear of forgetting my lines. This always applies when we are going out live, which we did with *Dixon* for seven years. It was murder. Nowadays the show is recorded and it is comforting to know that we can go back on a scene if necessary. But I still prefer to learn the script and be word-perfect before we begin.

The Huggetts on radio provided me with a memorably happy working period. During the whole of its nine years' run, I don't remember a moment of discord. I've been a lucky man and have always found myself working with friendly and good-natured people.

With a series such as the Huggetts, where the same people meet week after week year after year, it becomes very easy to go what I call sideways unless everyone is prepared to be co-operative. We had no tantrums with scripts being hurled across the studio or actors walking out in protest at some part of the dialogue they didn't like.

Little tiffs, of course, were written into the script from time to time, but we enjoyed these scenes and our dialogue promoted many a laugh after the broadcast had finished.

Kathleen is a wonderful person and artiste, extremely easy to work with and, so far as I'm concerned, as quick to raise a laugh with an audience as a tear.

The Huggett films, the radio series and *Holiday Camp* did a lot for Kathleen as they did for me. She had made countless stage appearances as a maid or a char, but she had not had an easy time. Kathleen married young and lived abroad with her husband for many years. When he lost his job she returned to England with their three children, and she and her husband were never reunited. She is now a widow. For years she combined her job of mother and housewife with that of actress, playing bit parts on the stage and in films. Most people think of her as the typical Cockney—an illustration of the realism she has brought to roles—but she was born in Lancashire and only came to London as a child when her father was appointed Borough Engineer of Southwark. She declared it was George Bernard Shaw who tipped her off on the best way to learn the Cockney accent. In her early days at the Royal Academy of Dramatic Art he advised her, 'Go into the Old Kent Road and just listen to the women talking.' Kathleen did—for hours on end—and it has paid off on those occasions when film folk were looking for someone to take the part of an East Ender.

Work became plentiful for her after the Huggetts and there was much more variety in the roles she was offered. She was absolutely first-rate in Noël Coward's *Nude with a Violin* in which she co-starred with Sir John Gielgud as a brassy dancing girl with a long line of lovers. I suppose it was inevitable that her greatest success would be achieved in a Cockney role—that of the char who inherited a fortune in the chart-topping television series, *Mrs Thursday*.

She is one of four actresses whom I consider know their jobs backwards and yet are entirely free of conceit. Gwen Watford, who graduated in the conventional way via repertory and also appeared in one of the *Dixon* series, comes into this category. And so does Celia Johnson, for whom I have an especial regard. The fourth is one of the real jewels of show business, Dame Edith Evans.

It was rather a sad day for Kathleen and myself when the Huggetts came off the air. It had been an extremely popular programme with an audience of ten million after its first month on radio. I doubt if many people will remember that Dick

Emery played some small parts in the series. Today I would rate him as my favourite comedian. Dick is among those comedians endowed with a lot of musical ability. He has a fine operatic voice and could easily have pursued a singing career.

During the late forties life became very hectic for me. I was dashing from one film studio to another in between broadcasting and also appearing in many variety shows. But of course, at the end of it all, the tax man cometh!

The work load was a little easier when I appeared in *It always Rains on Sunday* and *Against the Wind*, because although they were both produced in 1947 they were made at the same studios—Ealing. I had to dodge from one set to another, changing quickly from the role of a detective-sergeant to that of a murder victim, but at least I wasn't being type-cast!

In real life, I took on yet another role—that of interpreter when I nipped across to Brussels for their film festival and, because of my knowledge of French, was roped in to translate for many of the visiting stars.

It always Rains on Sunday was a film with plenty of action in it and, as is often the case, inspired everybody on the set and certainly excited the cast. The stars were Googie Withers—a woman of evergreen beauty as I'm sure millions of viewers of the television series *Within these Walls* will testify—and John McCallum. They became engaged during the shooting of the film and were married in January 1948, not long after its London première.

Early in her career Googie appeared in too many films as the dizzy blonde stooging for well-known comedians, until somebody rightly decided that she had undoubted straight acting ability and gave her a part in the wartime movie, *One of Our Aircraft is Missing*. She never looked back after this success and became one of Britain's best loved dramatic actresses in the post-war years, greatly in demand on the screen and in West End plays and television.

McCallum, too, did well in star roles for British studios, but ten years after their marriage he decided to exchange acting for theatre management in Australia, his native country. Googie completed a Shakespearian season at Stratford-on-Avon before flying out to join him and they have lived there with their family of three children ever since. But Googie has never stopped working and has enjoyed considerable triumphs not only in Australia but on Broadway. Happily, she occasionally returns to us to appear in television plays.

The whole action of *It always Rains on Sunday* took place on a wet Sunday in London's East End and here we had to go into reverse with the weather. While we shivered in the 'summer' in *Holiday Camp* we were now filming during a lovely dry spell, so the technical men had to get busy on the streets with hosepipes. Of course, the sun came out and dried the 'rain' so that many scenes had to be shot over and over again.

We were filming in the Leyton railway marshalling yards and I must say that I was most impressed with the way in which the yard master directed traffic. There are aspects of filming that are far removed from make-believe and one is made to realise this whenever a movie is authentically involved in the working lives of others. I picked up a lot of general knowledge on the subject in those days.

In my role as the detective, I had to run along the top of a moving train, jumping from carriage to carriage. I certainly couldn't do it now but at that time I found it quite exciting. In all the films I have made, I have only once used a double. This was due to some extent to pride and also because I never liked the thought of someone else being obliged to do the dirty work on my behalf.

One of the problems in filming the street scenes in *It always Rains on Sunday* was the disruption caused by hordes of East London kids. They were all over the place, crowding the cameras and getting beneath everybody's feet. However, when I wasn't required on the set, I persuaded them to join me in a quiet road for a sort of Garrison Theatre show with stories of my bike and reading letters from my brother Sid. Because of my own East End background, it wasn't difficult for me to tune in to their wavelength and anyway, I have always loved children and so has Mollie. It was a disappointment that our marriage was never blessed with some of our own.

Among those making their film debut in the production was Sidney Tafler, now a well-known actor. He played the part of a dance-band leader. We had a splendid cast of what I might call British film regulars, including Jimmy Hanley, that grand veteran, Edward Chapman, as well as Alfie Bass, Michael Howard, Susan Shaw, Jane Hylton, Hermione Baddeley and Gladys Henson. John Slater was making his first screen appearance after surviving an air crash at Le Bourget the previous year. He turned in a remarkable performance, despite a serious leg injury from which he had by no means recovered. More than twenty people were killed, and both John and his wife Betty, who had been holidaying in Paris, were badly injured but managed to escape from the blazing aeroplane. John had not long established himself as an actor and the crash could well have ended a promising career, but he is nothing if not a determined fighter and was filming again within seven months although with one of his legs still in irons. His wife, who filled in as his secretary, continued doing the job from a wheel-chair for a considerable time.

John Slater has long been familiar as Detective Sergeant Stone in '*Z*' *Cars* and as a story-teller on radio. In November, 1970, he was written out of the police series while undergoing a heart operation but nothing can subdue his indomitable spirit and he is as active as ever in the profession that he has made his own.

In my next film, *Against the Wind*, I swopped my exploits across the roofs of railway carriages for parachute jumping. The story was about six characters brought together on a sabotage mission to occupied Belgium, where we were supposed to be dropped. This involved some instruction at Heyford Parachute Training School, where we did everything except jump from an aeroplane which was not permitted. We were taken to the roof of a very high building, fitted with parachute harnesses, and then one by one launched off with a terrific swing from one side of a platform to the other preparatory to jumping at the right moment. I was not exactly bursting with enthusiasm and I discovered that the feeling was much worse than my experience of falling backwards and down one floor in *Hue and Cry*. The spring fittings on the harness stopped one from hitting the ground but it was distinctly unpleasant to see the ground rising to meet you. One minute I was on the platform and the next on the ground and I came to the conclusion it would have been marginally more pleasant to have jumped from an aircraft with ample time to float down rather than to land as swiftly as we did.

To meet some of the physical requirements of film-making I found it necessary to keep pretty fit and I've always endeavoured to keep my weight to reasonable proportions. I did once tip the scales at sixteen stones and decided to do something about it. Today I am careful about my alcoholic intake. Although I enjoy a drink I never use alcohol as a booster to be taken before a show, but I enjoy parties when the day's work is finished.

In *Against the Wind* I worked with that lovely and well-known French actress Simone Signoret, making her first appearance in a British film. She was then married to producer Yves Allegret and had a little daughter, Catherine, but a few years later she became the wife of Yves Montand, the internationally famous singer and actor. They are still together after more than twenty years and are held to be among the happiest couples in show business.

Simone is a quite remarkable woman. She never wears make-up, doesn't worry over-much about dieting, unless she is acting, and prefers sweaters and skirts or trousers to more glamorous trappings. She is an extremely positive person who has never been afraid of speaking her mind. For some time she was banned from radio, television and state-run theatres in France because she signed a manifesto supporting the right of Frenchmen to refuse military service in Algeria. She has nevertheless remained in the front rank of artistes in her professional association with such eminent co-stars as Sir Laurence Olivier, Sir Alec Guinness, James Mason and many leading French actors. She won an

Oscar for her wonderful portrayal of the abandoned mistress in *Room at the Top*, in which she played opposite the late Laurence Harvey.

It was almost an honour to be 'killed' by Simone when I played a traitor in *Against the Wind*. She was an A.T.S. girl who accurately fired at me with a revolver! Robert Beatty, who later became a close friend of mine, was among a cast which included John Slater, James Robertson Justice and Gordon Jackson.

The production of films based on several related stories became rather a vogue in the immediate post war period here and in America and *Easy Money*, which I made in 1947, was yet another. The theme involved football pool winners in four episodes, showing the effect of sudden wealth on four sets of characters. I played the father of a suburban family (I still have this father of the family tag and it seems to stick), Marjorie Fielding was my wife and young Petula Clark my daughter—as she was later in the Huggetts. Dennis Price and Greta Gynt, who were both with me in *Dear Murderer*, shared another episode as did Mervyn Johns and Edward Rigby.

I worked with Dennis Price in a number of films and the news of his death in a Guernsey Hospital in October, 1973, came as a shock. He was only fifty-eight and had been living in more or less self-imposed exile in the Channel Islands for about seven years to evade some of the burdens of income tax.

Price was one of the casualties of show business. A clever actor with a distinctive style, he was at one time at the very top of the profession, with a fan mail exceeding that of many leading Hollywood stars. He was earning a comfortable living and there seemed no reason why he should not have done so for as long as he wished but something went wrong. Quite suddenly he was no longer being offered the roles he was accustomed to receiving and then began a long depressing slide from which his career never recovered.

The son of a brigadier, Dennis decided he wanted to become an actor while still at Oxford and went straight from there to the

Embassy Theatre School. He appeared on the stage at the Croydon Repertory Theatre in 1937 and made his West End debut within a year. After serving with the Royal Artillery during the second war, he began his screen career, making more than fifty films, of which, I suppose, *Kind Hearts and Coronets* with Alec Guinness was probably the most noteworthy. Just before the war he had married Joan Schofield and the couple had two daughters, but the marriage was dissolved in 1950.

He then hit his really bad spell. People began asking the dreaded question, 'What's happened to Dennis Price, you never hear of him now. . . ?'

In 1954, overcome by depression, he made an attempt on his life but was rescued from a gas-filled room. It was ironic that this incident restored his name to the newspaper headlines and gave him the chance to work again. Suddenly he ceased to be a forgotten man, but his affairs were in a mess. He was made bankrupt on a demand for £10,000 unpaid tax and admitted spending more than £17,000 in two years on 'extravagant living and most inadequate gambling'.

Fortunately the financial cloud was dispelled when he was 'discovered' by television in the sixties as the inimitable Jeeves in the P. G. Wodehouse series, *World of Wooster*, with Ian Carmichael. His portrayal was truly delightful and immediately his old fans began writing to him again. But when the series ended he tended to make fewer and fewer visits to this country and little was heard of him. He had been in hospital nearly three months suffering from a broken hip when his death was announced.

I suppose it is inevitable that having spent nearly forty years in show business I should have to mourn the passing of so many talented people with whom I have worked during my career.

But when one has worked alongside so many accomplished actors and actresses their deaths create a vacuum for a long time and I feel that, in my story, I would not be doing justice if I omitted to mention them.

There is nothing quite as infectious as the sound of children's laughter and I love to be in their company when they are looking in on a television programme of vintage comedies. The broad humour that tickled us years ago has, of course, long been overtaken by sophisticated entertainment with a substantial measure of sexual allusion, but I am more than a little gratified to find that the kids really enjoy the old slapstick comedy that was a real art form in the early years of the cinema. Laurel and Hardy, Abbott and Costello and the riotous Marx Brothers may not always appeal to the adults of today but I get a devil of a kick out of watching children falling about with laughter whenever the old-time comics appear on the small screen.

I must confess, however, that I rather dread the resurrection on television of another film I made—*My Brother's Keeper*—in which I played the part of a killer. I'm afraid it really would wreck my Dixon image with the youngsters.

I was an old lag who had escaped from jail and would stop at nothing to retain his freedom. That was the only really vicious character I ever portrayed. George Cole—now a household name—appeared with me as a rather simple-minded lad to whom, for the purposes of the plot, I was handcuffed. No offence to George, but there are few things worse than being attached to someone for any length of time. They were only rubber handcuffs but we were both mighty glad when we could get rid of them.

George was a protégé of Alastair Sim—I believe he was evacuated to Alastair's cottage in Oxfordshire during the London blitz—and was given his first chance on the stage in a play called *Cottage to Let* in which Alastair was the star. George was only fifteen at the time but he notched up several stage and screen successes before he was called up for three years' service with the R.A.F.

My Brother's Keeper was one of the first of a large number of films George made for Rank after his return to civilian life. I was most impressed with the way he handled his part and not in the least surprised at his later successes. Many people will remember him as David Bliss, the amiable, bumbling hero of radio's *Life of Bliss*. The series ran for six years and was later transferred to television. He is now, of course, one of our best-known actors, one of his greatest triumphs being his portrayal of Max Osborne in the I.T.V. series, *A Man of our Times*.

I think that, contrary to my practice, I would have been well advised to use a double in *My Brother's Keeper*, because in one sequence I had to run in front of a moving train—which wasn't all that funny. When I discussed the scene with the train driver, he said, 'You're scared, aren't you?'

'I'm frightened to death,' I admitted. I knew that if he increased his speed even by a fraction, I could finish under the wheels. He smiled and assured me that he could handle the situation.

When we were watching the rushes the following day, someone suggested the sequence should be shot again but Sydney Box retorted, 'You bloody well won't do it again.' He had noticed the buffers had been unpleasantly close.

At the end of the film and as the murderer, I was stalked through woods by thirty policemen and blown up when I reached land that had been 'mined' for army manœuvres. I did have a 'double' for that scene or otherwise I shouldn't have lived to tell the tale. We used a dummy! I stood at a safe distance and watched it being blown into the air.

My next screen appearance was as the Governor of a Borstal institution in *Boys in Brown*, with a cast that included Dirk Bogarde, Richard Attenborough, Jimmy Hanley, Alfie Bass and Andrew Crawford.

Because I was already fully committed, I had to pass up the opportunity of appearing in *Passport to Pimlico*—the first of a marvellous series of delightful comedies to come out of Ealing Studios. It was followed by *Kind Hearts and Coronets* and *The Lavender Hill Mob*. Stanley Holloway took the part I was offered as the man who planned to make Pimlico an independent 'state' of London. As usual his performance was superb.

After *Passport to Pimlico* Stanley registered yet another outstanding success as Dolittle in *My Fair Lady*. I often wonder what direction my career would have taken had I opted to work on this particular film and not appeared in *The Blue Lamp*. The *Dixon* series might never have eventuated . . . it is interesting to look back on all the ifs and buts in one's life. In fact, later I had to miss the chance of playing Dolittle in the American production of *My Fair Lady*.

The film *Boys in Brown* once again emphasised my 'father' image and as the Borstal Governor I had to face the tricky problems that followed the recapture of an escaping gang of boys. I recall one very dramatic scene in which Bogarde, who had been beaten up by the rest of the gang and was terrified for his life, went down on his knees to me as he pleaded for protection.

The film, so far as my role was concerned, was made at Pinewood Studios, and this was something of a disappointment to me because I find location work with real scenery and backgrounds much more interesting and, for that matter, more inspiring to me as an actor.

I always liked to make an early start when I was filming and having arrived punctually for my call I hated killing two or three hours awaiting my summons to the set. An awful lot of time was, and doubtless still is, wasted because timing is badly organised, and time is money. One thing that always exasperated me was the frequent abrupt ending to a day's shooting. An actor or actress could be in the middle of a scene or even in the middle of a sentence, well into a part to which he or she had been warming all day and conscious of a certain amount of tension . . . then snap! The lights died. Everything was halted the very second the union officials told their men to pack up.

At 8.30 a.m. the following morning and back on the set again, one was expected to duplicate the mood that existed at the moment of cutting the day before, and that was not easy. The mood and the moment had been lost. Acting is not as simple as many people think. It takes time to get inside the skin of the character one is playing and it can't always be done to union rules.

I found the policy of having sometimes thirty or forty takes of one small scene, so the the best could be selected, equally irritating. I refused to accept that there was a best. I believed producers would have found their best had they rolled their cameras, without telling the players, at the penultimate rehearsal.

Everyone is familiar with the scene-stealing propensities of babies and animals and there is one story about an actor and a dog which always makes me smile. The dog had to enter the room and drop a newspaper at the feet of his master. He was well trained and played his part well, but unfortunately something went wrong with the cameras, then with the lights and later with the sound recording. The scene was shot fifteen times. 'Right,' said the director, 'we'll have one more go and this has got to be the one.'

For the sixteenth time, the dog came into the room and dropped the newspaper—then smartly nipped the actor's leg and scuttled off the set. Never let anyone tell me that animals haven't more sense than humans—I don't believe it!

CHAPTER 8

I Drive an Express Train

I WAS told I was the envy of every boy in Britain (and a good many chaps well out of their boyhood) when I made the film *Train of Events*, because I really did drive an express train.

When Sir Michael Balcon asked me if I would like to play the part of an engine driver in this film I replied that I would on condition that I was coached well enough to drive the express train properly. 'If I'm going to play this part I want it to be authentic,' I added.

Micky agreed and that was how I actually drove the Euston–Liverpool express out of Euston Station. Not very far and not very fast, I must admit, but nevertheless I did drive—and without slipping the wheels which, according to my tutor, was as common a fault with engine drivers under tuition as slipping the clutch is with the learner drivers of cars. Mind you, I was an amateur and remained an amateur. My teacher was a great big fellow named Ned Sparks who always wore a bowler hat. His name has always stuck in my memory because the only other Ned Sparks I ever heard of was the American movie comedian who always uttered his dry jokes in an unvarying monotone and usually chewed on a fat cigar.

As I stood in the cab with eighty-five tons of machinery pulsating in front of me and we took bends at speed, the monster looked more than a little awesome to me, but it was all a schoolboy's dream come true. Manipulating the mechanical mass, which professional drivers seemed to think possessed a soul, was absolutely fantastic.

On the initial journey to Liverpool, the train was driven by a little chap no more than five feet tall who sat on a stool. I need hardly say that the view from the footplate is vastly different from that one gets on a journey when looking out of a compartment window, or even standing on a station or from a road or field as the train goes by. As we approached Tring Tunnel at about seventy miles an hour, the mouth seemed so small that I said in alarm, 'It won't go through there.' The under-sized driver, who was looking out of the side of the cab, didn't bother to turn round. He just shouted over his shoulder, 'The old cow went through yesterday, guv'nor.'

In the meantime, Ned Sparks had handed me a duster which he told me to put over my face as we reached the tunnel. When we emerged, I asked him why the face protection had been necessary. 'Well,' he said, 'sometimes the windows in the side of the cab get a bit loose and with the vacuum created by the wind as we pass through the tunnel they may shatter so that the glass is thrown into your face. . . .'

Once again, *Train of Events* was something of an omnibus story—compressing several tales about different sets of characters on board the 3.40 p.m. express from Euston to Liverpool with the lives of everyone reaching a climax as the train crashes into a petrol tanker on a level crossing. The accident looked so realistic in the completed film that it was difficult to believe it hadn't really happened. It was a clever combination of model craftsmanship and actual wreckage. Once again, we were in the hands of technicians with expertise.

A studio team went from Ealing to Wolverton Carriage Works in Buckinghamshire and constructed a 'wreck' from old derelict railway stock provided by British Railways. They were assisted by railway officials well versed in the technicalities of crashed debris. The shooting of this sequence took three nights, with our technicians working from eight in the evening until seven o'clock the next morning. A hundred Wolverton people were engaged to play the roles of passengers involved in the crash and we used regular ambulancemen and rescue squads. A model train in Ealing Studios was brought into operation for the actual impact. It was quite small and was fixed to a table only a few feet wide, but by the time the genuine and the fake had been fused on film it was impossible for the eye to separate them. I tried to buy the model but the studio wouldn't sell and it's been used since in other films. Model boats are similarly employed for filming in the same way, but unless great care is taken, they are easily detected, especially if they are filmed in fresh water.

It was in this film that I nearly broke my back. The camera was in the driver's cab of the real train and I, as the driver, was wrenching on the brakes at the moment I sighted an obstruction on the track. Too realistically, I fell backwards and collided with solid iron. The hefty clout I took in the spine affected a leg and hip and this is the reason why, today, I sometimes suffer pain from arthritis when I'm walking.

The stupid and ironic thing about this regrettable incident was that it was deleted in the cutting room!

Leslie Phillips, familiar now to television audiences—and what a riot he was as the suave Casanova—gave a performance far removed from his customary light-hearted parts. He was the rescuing fireman, intensely worried and sympathetic, as he dragged me to safety from the crash.

Gladys Henson, my waiting wife in *The Captive Heart*, was again my waiting wife in this film and once more, Susan Shaw was my daughter. Valerie Hobson and John Clements contributed a delicious piece of light comedy. It was also Peter Finch's first film after he had been 'discovered' in Australia by Laurence Olivier. Peter had a small part as a chap who had murdered his wife (Mary Morris) and concealed her body in a

Father and Mother: Ted and Maud Waters.

As Churdles Ash in *The Farmer's Wife*.

3. A scene with Kathleen Harrison from the film *Holiday Camp* which led to the Huggett films and a radio series.

4. With sisters Elsie and Doris (Gert and Daisy) Waters.

The Huggetts on radio (1953). *Left to right,* Vera Day, Anthony Green and Kathleen Harrison.

Myself (*left*) with Jeff Darnell in cabaret (1935).

7. Seconds later I was shot dead by Simone Signoret in *Against the Wind*.

As P.C. George Dixon in *The Blue Lamp* which began my long Dixon career.

9. A charity cabaret in Jersey and a meeting with Princess Margaret (1959).

10. With the original *Dixon* team.

. There's nothing quite like summer at our Kent home.

12. Violette Szabo (Virginia McKenna) says goodbye to 'Father' before going on a mission to Occupied France during the war. A scene from *Carve Her Name With Pride.*

13. Presented to King George VI and Her Majesty. Others pictured include David Tomlinson, Jack Hulbert and Jean Simmons.

theatrical basket on the train. Joan Dowling was also in the cast.

I have to thank Micky Balcon for my long career as Dixon because it was he who first asked me if I would be interested in playing the part of the old copper on the beat in *The Blue Lamp*. Before I'd read the script, I hoped I would like it because I so enjoyed working with Micky. He was a producer who always would listen to an actor's opinion without flipping his lid. He was the opposite of a Mr Know-all and realised that the minor problems of his players on the set were rarely apparent to the men behind the cameras or squatting in the director's chair. I didn't have to read much of the script because after twenty minutes of filming, I was knocked off! But as I've stated earlier, a small part can sometimes overshadow a star part in importance.

Because I had played major roles in many other movies, a number of my friends advised me not to accept the Dixon part but I realised that the murder of the policeman, far from eliminating him, really gave him a martyr's crown as a man never to be forgotten and that any audience would readily understand the spirit of the film and the message it conveyed.

There had never been an authentic police film until the production of *The Blue Lamp* and until then celluloid policemen had mainly been comic characters with splayed feet who wore their helmets on the backs of their heads with chinstraps under their noses.

After I had agreed to play Dixon, those of us who were members of the 'force' were taught that there is a correct way of putting on the helmet—with two fingers beneath the peak and with the chinstrap just over the chin. We learned, too, the etiquette of the helmet. When calling upon someone, it may be held in the hand. On a social visit, however, the helmet is put down on a table except when calling upon a V.I.P., such as a bishop or politician, when it must be carried beneath the arm with the badge facing forward. These were small points but important ones—especially as it was anticipated the film would attract many audiences of real policemen.

Although the story was fictional the film was almost a documentary. It was made with the full co-operation of Scotland Yard and with the invaluable help of many members of the Metropolitan Police. The Commissioner in office, Sir Harold Scott, visited Ealing Studios to see rushes of some of the early scenes and on his advice any technical inaccuracies were corrected. Filming took place at several police stations but the focal point for the cameras was at Paddington Green—hence Dock Green—where Chief Inspector Wilkinson and his staff coached us in the manning of the station.

We had two other tutors from whom we received invaluable advice—Chief Superintendent Nobby Clark and Detective Chief Superintendent Jock Jamieson. Not surprisingly, there were occasions when the film coppers were mistaken for the real coppers. More than a dozen men in blue were milling around in the station's main corridor when Nobby Clark entered one morning. I was wearing my helmet according to regulations and had it pulled well down and he failed to recognise me. 'What's all this lark?' he barked. 'Why aren't you out on duty?'

I had twigged his mistake, of course, and just for the hell of it retorted, 'You shut up and mind your own bloody business!'

He could hardly believe his ears and was about to tear me off a colossal strip when the truth dawned on him. The story of that incident reverberated throughout the force.

To ensure the accuracy of every detail of police procedure, we had Inspector Leonard Pearcy, an instructor at the Peel House Training School, attached to the film unit as technical adviser. A car used in some of the early scenes was 'doctored' by Yard officers so that it looked like a real police car. In the final exciting cops-and-robbers chase, we were also allowed to use police radio cars. They were loaned on a carefully worked out availability rota.

Scenes of the activities at Scotland Yard's Information Room, where all 999 calls are received and communications maintained with and between radio cars, were filmed in short takes on two successive Sundays. The cameras panned in on genuine police officers—Inspector Law, P.C. King and P.C. Fleet, who were seen and heard sending radio messages to police cars in the final scenes of the film.

Yet another authentic touch was added when the script called for a stolen car to be examined for finger prints. The job was done by the late Detective Chief Superintendent Fred Cherrill, head of the Fingerprints and Photographic Department. He was helped, as he would have been on a real case, by Detective Superintendent Jack Livings. When we were filming night scenes in Paddington, the streets were first reconnoitred by officers to establish suitable locations. I think, in fact, there were probably more real policemen than actors in *The Blue Lamp.*

Inevitably, with all these genuine and make-believe coppers around, people in the street became a trifle confused. Jimmy Hanley was in several scenes with me—as the new recruit being shown the ropes by an old hand—and we were often stopped by people with problems on their minds. Fortunately we had become so familiar with the area that usually we were able to direct them to any street or building they were seeking. It was easier to do this and forget about the explanations concerning our real identities. But I did slip up badly on one occasion. I was walking towards a concealed camera—it was just a routine shot of the bobby on the beat—when a car drew alongside. The owner got out, stood directly in front of me and said, 'Excuse me, officer, is it all right for me to leave the car here while I have a spot of lunch?' Without thinking, and feeling a little put out because he had spoiled the shot, I replied 'It's nothing to do with me. You can leave it here all day as far as I'm concerned.' When I realised what I had probably let the poor fellow in for, I took off for Paddington Green Police Station to tell the real cops that it wouldn't be the driver's fault if somebody knocked him off for parking.

On another occasion there was a scene in which a police constable had to drag a 'drowning woman' from the Regent Canal. A passer-by who failed to notice the cameras promptly put in an emergency call for an ambulance. Embarrassed actor,

Meredith Edwards, had to explain to the mercy squad that he wasn't really a policeman and that the 'victim' had never been in danger of drowning.

There was a less amusing incident one night when we were shooting scenes outside a jeweller's shop. The camera lights were shining on the road as several of us, including real policemen, were standing around. Suddenly I saw a car approaching us at a hell of a speed and it appeared that the driver had not even seen us. Just before he reached the cameras he slammed on his brakes, opened his door and practically fell out of the car. He was fighting drunk and had a go at one of the real officers who questioned him.

The same episode produced one of the funniest little scenes in the film. A girl was taken to the police station to attend an identification parade and pretended she was going to pick out the man who had robbed the jeweller. She walked up and down the line, pursed her lips, raised her eyebrows and several times was on the verge of making a choice but ended by failing to identify any of the men on show. At a further stage in the investigation she was told that the pearls given to her by the jeweller, her boy friend, were not genuine but 'cultured'. The way that word was repeated, and the facial expression that accompanied it was very amusing indeed, but hardly surprising since the actress was none other than Dora Bryan.

The film players were well recruited and included Bernard Lee, as the detective-inspector and Robert Flemyng as his sergeant. Dirk Bogarde was the young thug who 'shot' me and his sidekick was Patric Doonan (the son of the famous music-hall comedian, George Doonan); Peggy Evans appeared as Bogarde's girl friend and once again Gladys Henson was cast as my wife. Gladys was a musical comedy star for many years before she became a character actress.

Tessie O'Shea appeared as herself in a couple of music-hall sequences, providing an alibi for Bogarde and Doonan after the cinema hold-up. Already known as 'Two-Ton Tessie', she saucily claimed that she was, 'A pretty substantial alibi.'

Basil Radford appeared in the film by accident! The unit was at work in a billiards hall near Piccadilly Circus when Basil looked in for a game—and found himself among a crowd of extras!

The director was Basil Dearden, with whom I had previously worked in *The Captive Heart* and *Train of Events*. He tragically lost his life in a car accident. Basil was involved in films for thirty years and had a wonderful gift for directing light entertainment. But he was never afraid of tackling controversial subjects and some of his later films were concerned with social problems to which the British cinema had long turned a blind eye. *Victim* was about homosexuality, *Life for Ruth* was centred on religious objections to medical treatment, and *Sapphire* was a story based upon colour discrimination.

It was tragically prophetic that his last film, *The Man who Haunted Himself*, was about a man who crashed on the M4 and was released only a few months before Basil himself was killed there in March, 1971. His car left the road, hit a signpost and burst into flames. Basil had married actress Melissa Stribling in 1947. A divorce petition was filed in 1965, but there was a last-minute reconciliation and the case was withdrawn. Basil was very proud of *The Blue Lamp* and not without good reason. In addition to breaking all manner of records here, it went round a good part of the world and was shown in many countries over a number of years. I saw it in France, Germany and Greece and then in Hong Kong, when I was returning to this country from Korea in 1951. I had never thought I would hear myself talking Chinese but I did!

Long before this oriental visit took place Mollie and I decided to have a greatly overdue holiday immediately *The Blue Lamp* had been completed. We motored to Athens and then went on to Glyfada and had hardly settled in our hotel before we heard a voice say, 'Hullo, Mr. Warner, have you come to see your film?' The owner was an executive from Pinewood Studios who told me that *The Blue Lamp* was being shown nearby. We went the following night and the cinema manager recognised me at once and showed us to two seats. When it came to the scene in which Dixon was dying in hospital, having been gunned down, an old lady in front of us began to weep. She was terribly distressed and was creating so much disturbance that the manager went over to her and whispered. The old lady turned around, looked at me and then began a fresh outburst of sobbing. The manager's assurance that I was very much alive and sitting in the seat behind brought her no comfort at all.

While I was immensely thrilled to be voted top British male star by the *Motion Picture Herald*, after *The Blue Lamp*, I received another award I treasured above everything! It was a casket and scroll presented to me by officers of the Metropolitan Police 'F' Division and gave me 'the freedom of police stations, the freedom of their tea, the freedom to criticise its quality and, if he does, the freedom of the cells'. This little tribute was made to me after the film's première by Chief Superintendent F. H. Archer, of Hammersmith, who had taught me how to walk, talk and salute like a policeman.

A couple of years after the film's first showing I was temporarily released from my contract with Rank to enable me to appear in a stage version of the story. Jack Hylton, who presented the show for a summer season at Blackpool and in 1952, at the London Hippodrome, made a characteristic decision about the casting.

'If Jack Warner is going to earn all that money,' he said (I had been offered a good salary plus a box-office percentage) 'then we're not going to have him shot in the first twenty minutes.' So, for the only time in the history of Dixon, I played a different role as Detective-Inspector Cherry (played in the film by Bernard Lee), which enabled me to survive until the final curtain and give Hylton his money's worth! That wonderful character actor Gordon Harker took the part of P.C. George Dixon. The late Bonar Colleano was the young thug who shot Dixon and Susan Shaw, his girl friend. Peter Byrne, who is, of course, still with me in Dixon, appeared for the first time as Andy Crawford. My old chum Arthur Rigby played the station sergeant as he did in the television series until his death.

We had two weeks at the New Theatre in Oxford before the sixteen-week season at Blackpool and subsequently appeared at the London Hippodrome, doing two shows nightly during its run. We used a revolving stage and in the final scene the whole theatre was involved in the action, with lights up and 'policemen' scouring the auditorium in their search for the 'killer'. It made the whole production quite exciting by giving the audience a sense of participation.

CHAPTER 9

With the Boys in Korea

My First Film in 1950 again offered me the challenge of a new characterisation. It was called *Talk of a Million* and was based upon Louis D'Alton's play, *They Got What They Wanted,* which had enjoyed considerable success at Dublin's Abbey Theatre. I had to play the part of an Irishman and it was absolutely imperative that my accent matched that of the other members of the cast who, needless to say, were nearly all Irish.

My old friend, John Paddy Carstairs, directed and I was aware that several people had expressed their doubts of my ability to sustain the Irish brogue throughout the picture. 'He's not just a Cockney,' Paddy sharply retorted, 'he's a versatile actor.' Paddy's defence sharpened my determination to justify the chance he had given me.

In other films I had experienced little difficulty in impersonating Lancastrians, Yorkshiremen and Scots and even a German professor in one of my monologues. But I had never played an Irishman before, although I reckoned that having an Irish grandmother, as I did, wasn't exactly a handicap!

I imagine that everybody has listened at some time in their

lives to the telling of an Irish story and squirmed at a performance that opened uncertainly in Connemara and ended in the Clyde.

What I was required to do was to achieve the authentic and I did not for a moment underestimate the task. I persuaded an Irish actor friend of mine, Michael Dolan, from the Abbey Theatre, to spend three weeks with us at our home in Kent.

Michael's help was invaluable and he taught me not only how to pronounce difficult words with an Irish inflection but also how to absorb the lilt of a language that, like the Welsh tongue, has its own music. I'm prepared to state, though, that I was extremely worried about my delivery and on reflection, I think I might not have taken the part so readily had I been appearing in a stage production where mistakes become infinitely more noticeable and cannot be corrected. I managed to get Paddy to give me an undertaking that if he detected the slightest change in my brogue, he would order a re-take. Fortunately, this only happened on rare occasions.

The plot was about an airy-fairy Irishman who kids his fellow villagers into believing he has inherited a fortune. As the unscrupulous but delightful boyo endowed with more Blarney than I have ever encountered in a genuine Irishman, I thoroughly enjoyed myself. Indeed, as I got into bed every night I could not but relish the prospects of the skulduggery I would be engaged in the following day.

Barbara Mullen was cast as my wife. I suppose many of the younger generation think of her as Scottish because of the part she has played in the long-running television series, *Dr. Finlay's Casebook*, but she is as Irish as Dave Allen and was a natural for the film. Others in the cast included another stalwart of the Abbey Theatre, Noel Purcell—we welcomed him in a Dixon episode a few years ago—Ronan O'Casey, Vincent Ball (an Australian with Irish parents) and Sid James.

An Irish brogue was not the only requirement for the part. I had also to start growing hair to over-run the short back and sides then in vogue. I thought this would be a simple matter

—just forget about visits to the hairdresser. But, oh no, as the young lads today can confirm. I spent more time in the barber's chair than I have ever spent before or since. It meant presenting myself at the studio daily two hours before filming so that a very fancy hair stylist could work on me with curlers, setting lotions, a dryer and, yes, the final humiliation for a man of my generation—a hair net!

I emerged with a lot of floppy, wavy locks which curled round my ears and cascaded over my eyes. Among the long-haired styles of the seventies such a coiffeur would pass unnoticed, but in the early fifties public reaction was rather different. I got a little tired of being whistled at by lorry drivers, bus conductors and passing youths. I was elated, I can tell you, when I was at last finally shorn!

Audiences would have watched the film happily convinced that they were viewing the green fields and stone walls of Ireland but, in fact, it was shot in the Cotswold village of Burford.

The only film in which I had to be assisted by a double—and I except the use of the dummy in the minefield—was *Valley of the Eagles*, made on location in Sweden and Norway. During the shooting, the cameras were drawn on sledges by a reindeer team. The rest of us, including the technicians, had to learn to ski to enable us to reach the set. I'm afraid I revealed very little ability. We arrived at a stage in the film, in which I played a Norwegian police inspector, when I was supposed to race down a mountainside on skis. Here a double had to be introduced and I must say I was delighted that this dangerous task was left to an expert.

Even if I had been sufficiently agile and proficient to be able to do my own thing, as it were, the studio would never have agreed. An injury to any member of the cast could have wrecked the entire schedule. There *was* an accident though, and the victim was Mollie. She was making her first screen appearance in a bit part and broke her ankle while attempting to ski. Other valuable studio properties with me in Sweden were John

McCallum, Nadia Gray, Mary Laura Wood, Anthony Dawson and Christopher Lee.

I wrote a little ditty to the tune of 'Me and my Shadow' about my double who was extremely impressive:

Me and my double skiing down the mountains wide,
Watching my police coat, no one knows that I am not
  inside.
When I see him ski so well
I'm very pleased 'cause no-one can tell
That it's only my double doing things that I can't do.

Compared with the climatic conditions in which we made this film, the *Holiday Camp* sequence with Kathleen Harrison at Lime Grove Studios was made in a heatwave! For a great part of the time, we were working outdoors in a temperature of twenty-five degrees below zero. It wasn't so bad when shooting took place in the cities but we ran into some uncomfortable blizzards at Nystuen, 5,000 feet up on the Norwegian mountains. In spite of the weather difficulties, Nat Bronsten, the producer, maintained his eight-week schedule, even though it sometimes meant filming far into the night. And some people think that being a film star is a fantastically glamorous business!

The only time our schedule was in real jeopardy occurred when we 'lost' 500 reindeer. The animals had been rounded up ready for the cameras but suddenly got stage fright and bolted into the mountains.

We had to call in a spotter aeroplane and when the pilot located them herdsmen were sent to round them up. Some had travelled more than sixty miles from the shooting scene.

During this film I drove one of the oddest vehicles I have ever encountered. I had handled horses and all types of cars, including the powerful machines I raced at Brooklands, and, of course, had managed a brief session as master of the Euston–Liverpool express, but the contraption with which I was confronted in *Valley of the Eagles* was a rum job called a pulka. It was shaped like the prow of a canoe and was just about as comfortable. It was drawn by a single reindeer and controlled only by a thin piece of rope which one had to crack against the animal's legs. Sometimes the reindeer took exception to this treatment and became frisky so that the driver was in some danger of losing his dignity and being catapulted backwards into the snow. Rudolph, as my reindeer was inevitably christened, scorned such directions as 'Gee-up' and 'Whoa, boy', and would neither start or stop until I made the right sort of deep rumbling noises.

When filming finished, we brought Rudolph back to England with us and presented him to the London Zoo. He was a fairly friendly animal and we thought he might be happier among people rather than with the herd. For a while, he was in pets' corner at the Festival of Britain in Battersea Park, where he became popular with the children.

In 1951 I received a call from Alastair Sim, asking me if I would join him in the cast of *Scrooge*, a new version of Dickens' story to be made by Renown Pictures. Alastair was playing the title role and he wanted me for the part of Mr. Jorkins. It wasn't a major role but I didn't mind that because working with Alastair was always fun.

We had a strong cast, with Kathleen Harrison as Mrs. Dilber, Mervyn Johns and Hermione Baddeley as the Cratchits, plus Miles Malleson, Ernest Thesiger and Clifford Mollison.

The film won the Blue Ribbon Award of America's Screen Council—presented for films of outstanding merit and for its suitability as family entertainment. Alastair, Kathleen and I were presented with Blue Ribbon plaques.

Times have greatly changed. Nowadays anything goes, and far from producers striving to make pleasant family features there appears to be fierce competition to see who can launch the nastiest film for public delectation. I have a lot of sympathy for parents who so often search in vain for suitable cinema programmes to which they can take their children—especially during school holidays. I know some horror and sex films bring a flood of coins to the cash registers so that some film distributors can laugh all the way to the bank but at the risk of being condemned as old fashioned I still believe that players, film-makers and distributors have a duty to the public as well as to their bank managers. I don't pretend that it would be practical to turn out movies that would create financial problems but I am convinced that there still exists a massive demand for good family entertainment that is not being satisfied.

So-called permissiveness has tended to become a euphemism for plain unadulterated filth. Everybody knows what is beneath a skirt and inside a pair of trousers. There's nothing new about sex and I can't understand why it is presented as a discovery on a par with that of North Sea gas.

The quality of television entertainment has similarly deteriorated. I have seen fellow artistes I've known and worked with for years suddenly appearing in doubtful productions and for one reason only—the fear of unemployment! The more infectious this becomes the greater will be the degeneration in the standards of entertainment.

It is astonishingly difficult to comprehend the reason for this trend when we so often find that television ratings constantly show that the most popular programmes are those light-hearted and almost sexless comedies such as *Bless This House*, *My Wife Next Door* and Wendy Craig's *Not in Front of the Children* and *Mother Makes Three*. If the public really wanted sex so much and the kitchen sink sagas I don't believe we would have fifteen million people watching each episode of *Dixon* and similar family programmes.

I am certain there would be a warm and friendly welcome today for films possessing the quality of the old Ealing Studio comedies. There is more than enough drama, tragedy and violence in real life to make all of us grateful for the therapy of laughter in these grim times. The late Walt Disney realised the need for this release from care as much as anyone and deserves the special place he has in the annals of international entertainment.

My sisters, 'Gert and Daisy', have not varied their act, only its content, during all their years in the business and today when they appear in summer shows here, or abroad, the fun they generate among responsive audiences is as wholesome as it ever was.

It is a sobering thought that so-called permissiveness and the collapse of moral values propelled the downfall of the Roman and Greek empires.

Almost without exception members of my profession have at some time or other entertained troops, and here again it is difficult to understand why certain comedians take it for granted that a service audience must be regaled by risqué material. They tend to forget that servicemen are only civilians in uniform and are well capable of judging the quality of an act. They realise, too, that in trying to raise a laugh with one dirty joke after another the comedian is really talking down to them.

I never found it necessary or desireable, to engage in smut when I went to entertain the lads in Korea in 1951. I gave them popular songs, sketches, stories, monologues and my Maurice Chevalier impressions and found them very appreciative.

Our chief problem was not that we couldn't raise a laugh from the boys who spoke English, but in trying to amuse those members of the United Nations Force who did not speak our tongue. I took my pianist, Bobby Alderson, with me and also a versatile chap called Jack Rogers.

We went at the request of George Brightwell, chief of Combined Services Entertainment at the War Office, and we were, in fact, the first contingent of British entertainers to visit Korea.

My agent, John McMichael, accompanied me—and wasn't I glad that he did! He was a very knowledgeable asset because he watched every move I made, advised me on such things as acoustics and was my 'minder' when I was invited to the mess for drinks. As I have mentioned before, I enjoy a drink but it would have done me no good at all to take a lot of alcohol after doing three shows in the heat of the day and necessitating three changes of clothing. Frequently John surreptitiously topped up my glass with soda water and my hosts were happy enough because they thought I was being tanked up with gin. They were guilty only of extending too much goodwill and generosity —bless 'em!

In six weeks we travelled 24,000 miles and entertained 24,000 troops at forty different shows. Sometimes there were as many as 3,500 men in the audience, while on other occasions, at isolated outposts, we put on exactly the same show for less than a dozen chaps. The three daily shows were often given at places many miles apart. I received wonderful support from the concert parties of the British 28th and 29th Brigades.

On the way to Korea we stopped over to give a show at Ibisu Camp, Tokyo. When we arrived we were met by four Japanese film actresses, each carrying a posy of flowers as a goodwill token, and afterwards provided with a sumptuous dinner at a private house. Of course, we had to remove our shoes before entering the house, in accordance with Japanese custom. This was quite relaxing but I wasn't exactly enamoured with their other custom of sitting on the floor. Just try eating roast beef, lobster and a variety of oriental delicacies with chopsticks while squatting cross-legged on a small cushion and you will get my point!

We gave our first two shows at Seoul before starting to move up the lines. What do you think I found when I showed up? My own tent with a small bicycle alongside bearing the notice, 'Mind my Bike!' Memories are made of this!

As we were preparing to leave after the show, we were surprised to see the band of the First Republic of Korea in a parade and heading in our direction. The bandsmen were accompanied by about fifty Korean children and the 'Mayor' and 'Mayoress', who accompanied them, were quickly unmasked as a couple of British Tommies who had come to thank us for entertaining them. I was very touched when each child handed me a bunch of flowers and joined together in the singing of 'Auld Lang Syne'—in Korean.

I certainly experienced some extremes of weather that year. In Norway and Sweden we had been practically frozen to death and in Korea it had been incredibly hot or unbelievably wet. I still don't know which was worse. When it was dry in Korea it was so dusty that vehicles had to drive with headlights blazing in daylight to see through the stuff, impenetrable as any old-fashioned London fog, and when it rained—oh my! It came down like steel stair rods! The heavens opened one night as I was doing a show on an outdoor stage so I shouted to the lads, 'What do you want me to do?'

They yelled back, 'Carry on, Jack, carry on.' Four soldiers held two ground sheets over Bobby, the pianist, to keep him and the piano dry and the boys in the audience huddled beneath ground sheets. My only worry was my suit. There were restrictions on the amount of clothing we were allowed to carry around so I nipped under cover, left the suit and completed my act in vest and pants. I finished the hour-long show drenched from head to foot, but at least I had preserved a good suit to wear another day.

I was reminded of this incident quite recently when travelling by train. After taking my order, a dining-car attendant startled me somewhat when he said solemnly, 'The last time I saw you, Mr. Warner, you were only wearing your pants.' Yes, he was one of the lads in that audience and had evidently not forgotten my strip tease act.

At a show in the American sector I was told by an officer, 'We didn't want to leave anything to chance so we double-checked the ground on which you will be giving your show. Would you believe it, we found another seven mines—one of them just at the back of the stage.' I must confess I was slightly uneasy in case he had overlooked a number eight! Out there I was prepared to believe anything.

I had played to American audiences in England and have to admit that they didn't always understand our peculiar brand of humour, but I seemed to get on their wavelength in Korea and the show went very well. The Americans certainly believe in home comfort abroad and I couldn't help grinning when I saw how thrilled out of their minds they were by the arrival of a giant refrigerator which held a few tons of ice-cream!

One of my last shows was put on for the 22nd Royal French Canadian Regiment, but here I had no language problem. I chatted to the lads in French and sang in both English and French. This proved to be the noisiest show of the tour because shells were bursting not more than a few hundred yards away and I had to bellow even louder in an attempt to overcome the competition from twenty-five pounders. Sitting in the audience was an officer equipped with a walkie-talkie which he used to keep in touch with men on outside patrol.

At one stage during the show, this officer asked me to stop singing for a moment while he called out the names of a dozen men. These chaps quietly rose from their seats and disappeared. A little more than an hour later six of them returned and resumed their original places just as unobtrusively. I was terribly shocked when I heard later that the other six boys had been killed on the patrol. So little time had elapsed between their laughing and applauding, and their call to duty when they unknowingly hurried out to their deaths. Fear for my own safety and that of the troops became very real to me when I noticed some Korean soldiers in battle order poking their heads through the back of the stage behind me. 'This is it,' I thought. 'They're here!'

I felt a bit of a fool but very relieved when I was told that they were South Korean fighters who had decided to take a brief break from battle to sample my entertainment. The trouble from my point of view was that all Korean soldiers, whether the enemy from the north or allies from the south, looked terribly alike.

My most embarrassing moment during the six weeks' tour occurred when we were returning to Tokyo after a visit to Kure, where we had entertained soldiers in hospital. Part of this journey had been made by flying-boat. I don't know if it was the actual flight, the heat or the food, but on the last lap of the trip, in a car with a Japanese driver, I realised that my stomach was gurgling like a waste pipe. I was in urgent need of a lavatory. I told John McMichael of my problem! Unfortunately, Japanese highways are not exactly lavish in public conveniences and I doubt if we could have identified one had we seen it, but John had a sudden inspiration. The one Japanese word John knew was 'banjo', which he was sure had nothing to do with a musical instrument but had some affinity to a Japanese loo.

John tapped the driver on the shoulder and shouted urgently, 'Banjo!' It worked. The driver halted the car outside a small private house. A woman came to the door, but because I knew I was then in *extremis*, I rushed past her. To my horror she shouted something I didn't understand and ignoring my desperate cries of 'Banjo', she pointed to my feet. I still didn't catch on until she lifted one of my feet and tried to remove my shoe. I suddenly realised that I was about to commit the unforgiveable sin of entering a house without discarding my shoes. I kicked them off in record time. Gee whiz! It was a close thing!

My recollection of that incident reminds me of another earlier occasion when I had similar trouble. It was way back in November, 1915, when I was one of five hundred members of the Royal Flying Corps on a short physical training course at The Curragh, in Ireland. We were lined up on church parade one Sunday morning when I suddenly felt terrible. I told the chap next to me that I thought I was going to faint and that he had better summon the sergeant. The sergeant, an ex-Guardsman with a big waxed moustache, was one of the real old school, and sticking his face into mine bellowed, 'And what's the matter with you?' I timorously told him I didn't know what was wrong but that I felt unwell. I suppose he thought I was lead-swinging and ordered me to stay where I was and then carry on with the others to church.

At that precise moment I knew why I had been feeling rotten. But it was too late! I had only just returned from France, where I had been attached to the French Army as driver and interpreter and again I think I suffered because of the change of food and air. I now recall the occasion with horror because I was forced to take part in the church service, singing 'Fight the Good Fight' with gusto, but the boys around me suffered! I was so ashamed of the occurrence that it was seven years later before I could bring myself to tell the story to my own brothers.

As we were leaving Korea, I had a brief meeting with Jack Benny and Errol Flynn. They had just arrived to entertain the boys, but we had no time for more than an exchange of greetings. Flynn was confident that he had met me in New York some years earlier and seemed a bit disappointed when I told him he was mistaken because I had never been there. I thought he was a very charming and friendly chap.

On our way home we did some concerts for the boys in the Suez Canal zone and then a show for the 'locals' in a Cairo cinema. Once again I faced a mixed audience. Some of them understood English, so I compromised by singing songs both in English and French and was then shocked by a terrific outburst of hissing. When I stopped singing so did the hissing but when I resumed, it began again. I could not help thinking that if destiny had decreed that Jack Warner should flop it was better that it happened in Cairo rather than London. I'll never know how I finished the act. Nothing like that had ever happened to me before. I did not know what to expect when the manager came rushing towards me. I was prepared for anything—except for what actually happened. To my amazement he flung both arms round my neck and cried, 'Wonderful, wonderful!'

Absolutely dumbfounded, I said, 'But—but, I don't understand. Why were they all hissing me?'

He beamed. 'That's not hissing the way you think of it. They hiss when they're pleased.'

We all live and learn, I suppose, trite though the phrase may be, but I wished that someone had warned me before I stepped in front of fifteen hundred people waiting to hiss!

I have always said that the Korean trip was one of the most worthwhile things I have ever done and I wished that I could have stayed longer with the boys out there, but there were film and other commitments awaiting me at home so I had to return.

The next British entertainer to go to Korea was Brian Reece, who had such a big following as radio's P.C. 49. He was succeeded by Ted Ray and then gradually other teams of artists made the tour.

Brian's career was ended by his untimely death at the age of forty-eight when he was at the peak of his career. He first reached the top in 1947 when he was given the lead in Cochran's West End production of *Bless the Bride*. Then came the radio series, which ran for six years with Brian as Police Constable Archibald Berkeley-Willoughby, otherwise P.C. 49—as popular in his day as I like to think Dixon is now.

He faced some of the problems I have experienced. So many people thought of him as a genuine copper that he had to be more than ordinarily careful about his private behaviour. Thousands of people all over the country are daily nailed for speeding without their offences meriting a line in the newspapers, but when P.C. 49 was caught and fined three quid he made headlines in nearly every national newspaper. I can imagine how he felt about it.

He continued his successful career on the stage, television, radio and in variety until he became very ill early in 1961. He suffered from a disease which turned his bones brittle and thus caused them to break very easily. Although frequently in great pain, he refused to give in. At one time he was in hospital for several months but soon after he was discharged managed to get about again and played a part in *The Seven Year Itch*—a play in which he had already appeared. Two hours before he was due on stage he cracked a hip bone and was rushed to hospital but refused to let the rest of the company down and went on stage in a wheelchair.

One of Brian's last appearances was as a member of the audience at a show to aid army charities. He worked on the script and collaborated with Harry Secombe in its organisation. By the time the big night came, with the Duke and Duchess of Gloucester as guests of honour, Brian was in Westminster Hospital. Again his determination triumphed over his physical weakness. He was taken to the Victoria Palace by ambulance and watched the show from his wheel chair in the aisle. He continued to make his weekly broadcast for B.B.C.—*Movietime*—from his hospital bed until his death in April, 1962.

I have never ceased to wonder at the great fortitude of so many of my friends on being stricken by desperate illnesses. As a witness to their courage, I have always felt most humble and Brian made me feel very, very humble indeed.

CHAPTER 10

Royal Variety Performance

UPON ARRIVAL home from the Korean tour in August, 1951, I returned to work in the studios. I played in three more films: *Emergency Call*, Noël Coward's *Tonight at 8.30* and *Those People Next Door.*

I again assumed the role of a detective in *Emergency Call*, the first of three films in which I was directed by Lewis Gilbert. I found him quite unlike any other film director I have known, quiet and easy-going, and softly spoken, but a man always capable of persuading his cast to go along with him. If any of the players appeared to get up-tight, Lewis would amble over to them murmuring, 'It will be all right when it's finished, let's all take it easy while we're doing it. . . .'

The other films we made together were *Albert R.N.* in 1953 and *Carve her Name with Pride*, several years later, and Lewis Gilbert certainly made all my working days very pleasant.

A child doomed to die within a few days unless someone with her rare blood group could be located formed the dramatic story line of *Emergency Call*. As a Scotland Yard inspector, I was in charge of the life and death hunt for the donor. Freddie Mills, who had been light-heavyweight champion of Great Britain, was appropriately cast as a boxer, but it was the memorable performance turned in by that wonderful coloured actor, Earl Cameron, that made the greatest impression on me. The handsome, suave Anthony Steel had the part of a young doctor.

Tonight at 8.30 was the film version of three marvellous one-act plays by Noël Coward and I had a relatively small part in one entitled *Ways and Means*. Valerie Hobson and Nigel Patrick were cast as a couple of upper-crust paupers trying to recoup their fortunes on the Riviera and I thoroughly enjoyed myself as a somewhat unconventional valet. In the other two plays, the leads were taken by Ted Ray and Stanley Holloway.

I made so many films during those days that my recollections of some of them are, inevitably, extremely sketchy, but I have retained one very vivid memory of *Those People Next Door*. Anthony Newley, then a complete unknown, had his first part, a small one, in this picture and because he had so little to do, was forced to spend a great deal of time mooching about the studio. Not an uncommon situation as I have said before. Some actresses kill time by knitting, but more often than not everybody drinks gallons of tea or coffee and lounge about bored to the eyeballs. Not the young Anthony! When he wasn't wanted, he eventually decided to stretch out on the floor in some studio corner and go soundly to sleep. I have never possessed the nerve to attempt such a thing simply because I don't have the ability to relax in this way. Tony was an extremely amusing boy and it was obvious he was very talented, but with the industry in decline, it would never have occurred to me to predict the great future that Tony has ensured for himself as film producer, writer and comedian.

Gladys Henson was with me yet again in what was a broad comedy about the fortunes and misfortunes of next-door neighbours, but on this occasion I was 'married' to Marjorie Rhodes and Gladys was the wife of the chap next door.

I have to make a frank confession that may horrify the Lord's Taverners in respect of my next film. It was called *The Final Test* and was entirely devoted to the sacred game of cricket, a sport which has never interested me in the slightest. I didn't play the game at all after leaving school and here I was cast as a great cricketer making his last appearance in an England–Australia Test match at the Oval. I had always regarded cricket as a game that provided too little action for players and spectators, yet I've known many chaps who have shirked work and pinched time off to watch matches that have been almost as important to them as the Battle of Britain!

For this reason I was very doubtful about accepting the part because I thought I would be unable to do justice to it, but I followed my usual practice of reading the whole script before coming to a decision and to my surprise, I discovered that it was a rattling good story and very human. I must admit, though, that I was more interested in the character as an ordinary man rather than as a cricketer.

Having decided to accept the role, I was anxious to turn in a believable performance, so I went to the cricket school run by ex-fast bowler Alf Gover and he really put me through my paces. I will admit that until then I had little understanding of how thoroughly cricketers prepared themselves for the sport. I didn't learn to love the game but at least I was groomed sufficiently well to act like a man who did.

The film was an adaptation of the play by Terence Rattigan and was directed by Anthony Asquith. The combined talents of both was a sufficient guarantee for the promotion of a successful movie. It had other attractions in the presence of England's most famous cricketers of the period—Len Hutton, Dennis Compton, the Bedser twins (Alec and Eric), Jim Laker, Cyril Washbrook and Godfrey Evans. All except Len Hutton appeared as themselves.

Len, England's captain, played the role not as himself but as a certain Bill Jarvis, and he had quite a lot of lines to learn. We rehearsed one scene for at least two hours, but in making his first appearance before the cameras Len was terribly nervous—who wouldn't be? After several retakes, made necessary because Len had fluffed his lines, I resorted to an old trick which often produces results. I went confidently into my part of the dialogue and then deliberately muffed it to ensure that yet another re-take was required. In addition I gave myself a roasting as the pro who had dropped a clanger and then turned to Len and said, 'Never mind, I've got it out of my system, Len, that goes for you too. Now let's start again and do it properly.' We began afresh, and, as I had anticipated, Len showed much more confidence and all went well. Anyway, how could we really expect him to do a first-rate acting job—it would have been as unrealistic as looking to me to play a faultless innings?

The dashing Dennis Compton was a much different proposition. He possessed nothing of Len's shyness and diffidence. He was the complete extrovert, to the great delight of cricket enthusiasts everywhere who admired his boldness and skill as one of the great batsmen of the post-war period. If he hadn't chosen cricket as a career, I'm sure he would have succeeded as a professional actor. He was handsome—many must remember his well-brushed appearance on bill posters advertising a certain hair cream—always immaculate and gifted with a ready wit.

Dressing me in white flannels and putting a bat in my hand didn't make me a cricketer and I was uncomfortably conscious of this in the presence of sporting top-liners, but they were a great crowd to work with and I learned what that overworn cliché, team spirit, really meant.

Once again the technicians worked a bit of a fast one on the audience because the film was not shot in the brilliant sunshine which magically appeared on the screen, but inside Pinewood Studios in the middle of winter and beneath terrifically powerful lighting. Shots from newsreels, a realistic backcloth and accurate reproductions of the Oval balcony and dressing-room made the whole set appear authentic.

One thing that was genuine was the unmistakable voice of commentator John Arlott. I think the only man who could have impersonated him was that master of a million voices, Tony Fayne, who had often imitated him on radio. How many people remember, I wonder, the music-hall duo of Tony Fayne and David Evans?

Although the activities of famous cricketers were an integral part of the film, the main theme was related only incidentally to the game and was much more a study of human relationships. As the ageing cricketer I was to become bitterly disappointed with my only son, who preferred poetry to sport and could not be troubled to visit the Oval on the occasion of his father's final appearance in a Test match. The difference in the temperaments and, indeed, in their outlook on life, is made clear on the morning of the match when at breakfast the father asks his son, played by Ray Jackson, to attend the all-important game. He shrugs off the invitation and woundingly describes the sport 'as knocking a bit of leather about with a piece of wood'. The father is aghast at this irreverence and can only remain silent in a very moving scene as the son leaves the house to visit a poet whom he greatly admires. Happy endings were imperative in those days and the trick is turned when the poet reveals his regard for willow-wielding and rushes the boy to the Oval to see his father in action.

Romantic parts were never really my forte, but in this picture it was decided that as the 'retiring cricketer' was a widower the human relationships would be incomplete for audiences if I didn't find a 'wife', so I had to fall in love. Hence the introduction of Brenda Bruce as a charming barmaid to whom I proposed marriage.

The poet, a delightful eccentric who wore boiler suits with a schoolboy cap and drove a handsome Bentley, was played by none other than Robert Morley for whom the part was absolutely tailor-made. I greatly value my long-standing friendship with Bob, with whom I came into close association in 1955, when I played the lead on tour in his comedy *Hippo Dancing*. Bob wrote the play and took over the title role of a loud-mouthed, dogmatic character in its London run of more than a year. Following him was not an easy task but audiences in the provinces were more than kind to me.

Simple incidents—and in this case an accident—can throw an actor off balance during a stage production. When I made my first entrance in this play at the Streatham Hill Theatre I stormed on to the stage and slammed the door—according to plan. It was then I realised I'd split the top of my thumb on a razor-like screw protruding from the door-knob. It was just not on to break off the dialogue and explain my predicament to the audience, so I had to thrust my hand into my pocket, bury my thumb in a handkerchief, and play on for an hour!

Pauline Jameson was my French wife in *Hippo* and Derek Waring, who has done so well in '*Z*' *Cars*, took the part of my son. There was keen competition for the role of my mother in the play, and I was seated in the stalls when the auditions were held. I heard a voice off stage and immediately said to myself, 'That's the one. . . .' I hadn't caught as much as a glimpse of the actress but I knew that the owner of the voice had to be right for the part. She was too—it was Evelyn Kerry, a lovely actress and a delightful little old lady. I often took lunch and tea with her while on tour and found her quite amazing, lively, energetic and possessing a magnificent sense of humour. She was then at least seventy-five!

On this tour I recaptured some of the happy family spirit which existed among the *Garrison Theatre* team. It was very different from the impersonal atmosphere of film studios where players are thrown together for a month or two. On the completion of a film many tentative arrangements are made to renew friendships at an early date, but they rarely materialise because artistes move around quickly from one studio to another, or even return to the stage. In a company on tour, everybody works together for months and is able to spend much more leisure time with each other, so that closer associations are forged.

Variety produces the same sort of friendships—especially if one frequently shares a bill with the same performers. You know, for instance, that when you are going to Liverpool you are going to say to each other, 'Wonder what the first house is going to be like?' Everybody is aware, of course, that it is always a tricky occasion on Merseyside. But there exists a sense of comfort in knowing that everybody faces the same task of winning the audience over having shared good audiences as well as bad.

Tom Walls was very conscious of the absence of audience communication when he started in movies. He was used to live applause and in one of his early films actually paused as he would have done on the stage, for the plaudits to cease. In films the technique is entirely different but a comic has always to work on the assumption that the audience won't laugh at his gag made before the cameras and has to keep the pace going. If the sequence is funny and members of the audience prolong their merriment, and thus miss another gag, they just have to catch up.

From the 'cricket pavilion' of Pinewood I went to the 'boxing arena' of Ealing where I had yet another part with a difference in *The Square Ring*. Basil Dearden directed and Robert Beatty played a veteran boxer trying to make a come-back.

Bob is a very forthright character and believes in calling a spade a spade. Like most of us in the profession he knows what it is to be unemployed, but he would never describe it as 'resting', the stage euphemism. He always says quite bluntly that he is or has been out of work! Fortunately, he doesn't have too many of these periods and has been more than gainfully employed since the time he chucked his job as a gas-meter reader in Hamilton, Ontario, and came to Britain as an actor in 1937.

George Rose, well known as an Old Vic actor, gave an excellent and very realistic performance as a punch-drunk boxer constantly trying to get back in the ring, and Maxwell Reed played the part of the bent young boxer who had sold himself to racketeers. Joan Collins and the late Kay Kendall were two of the few women in this picture.

People have such mixed feelings about boxing that I wouldn't care to decide whether this particular film was good or bad for the sport. I suppose it is rather a vicious game, but I think it's a good idea for young lads to be taught the art of self-defence while still at school, especially in these days of mugging and hooliganism.

Some young fellows I know were out driving one evening with their girlfriends when they were halted by a posse of thugs spread right across the road. They clearly intended to hand out a beating but were, of course, unaware that two of their intended victims were karate experts. The pair dealt effectively with the mob and then presented them to the local police. I'm always pleased when I hear of bully-boys being given a taste of their own medicine!

To cite yet another example that in film business one can learn a lot about other people's jobs, I found that in the fight game, although the professionals liked the money success brings, most of them really enjoyed their 'work' and were most unlikely ever to settle contentedly in regimented jobs that were safe but boring.

When one considers the number and variety of the films I have appeared in over many years, it seems that I have been singularly fortunate with those directors I have worked under, because I know that all too frequently here and elsewhere the most unholy rows blow up between directors, producers and stars. I have heard of actors and actresses in this country being bawled at and told, 'You are getting a hell of a lot of money and you're here to do as you are told.' Such situations never occurred when I was on a set. It would be wrong to pretend that some directors weren't tough—they were. But then that is their job. I was always willing to listen because I knew that the picture they had from the rear of the camera was altogether different from what I saw as an artist. Ultimately, too, one had to remember that if a film was a flop and lost money, the directors and producers, as well as the players, had to carry the can.

Human nature being what it is, it would be strange if some artistes were not spoilt by success. There were those who no longer troubled to see the rushes of the films they were making and had become either too big for their boots or convinced that they could not perform other than immaculately. For one reason or another, they displayed deplorable judgment. I was always keen to see the rushes because frequently I spotted minutes of film where my interpretation of the part could be improved.

Lewis Gilbert directed me for the second time in *Albert R. N.* which was produced by Danny Angel. Danny contracted poliomyelitis while in the army and was invalided out but refused to allow his handicap to wreck his movie career and did much of his work from a wheel chair. He and Gilbert were a great team.

Many televiewers will be familiar with this picture because it has been shown on both channels a number of times. It was, of course, another prisoner-of-war film and the setting was similar to that of *The Captive Heart.* The unit tried to find a prison camp, as they had done for the first film, but by the time *Albert R. N.* was conceived, in 1953, the camps had been cleared. Again the technical boys came to the rescue and built a wonderful replica. Anyone not in the know would have sworn that it was the real thing but it was actually built on the Surrey Hills near Dorking. We were on location for three or four weeks and such was the atmosphere of the place that we felt we were really prisoners. I can't adequately explain it, but the most terrible sense of oppression came over us as soon as we entered the camp and heard the gate clang behind us.

Although the setting was a mock-up, the story was authentic. There were some fictional touches, of course, but the main theme was based on events which actually took place at Marlag, Westertimpe. The 'Albert' of the title was a dummy cleverly constructed by John Worsley, the artist who had been a prisoner at the camp and whom I had met there when we made *The Captive Heart.* Worsley used what sparse materials he could scrounge and carried out an ingenious improvisation job. By using newspapers and bits of wire he accomplished the herculean task of creating a body. Two halves of a table-tennis ball helped create the figure's eyes and clippings of real hair from the camp barber thatched the head. When ten men were marched out of the camp for their weekly bath at the washhouse about half a mile away, one would remain behind in the ablutions to make his escape after dark. With the assistance of Albert, the dummy, who had been smuggled out in pieces hidden in the prisoners' towels and carefully assembled in the washhouse, ten men would be counted when they passed the guard on the return journey.

The lads held their breath a number of times, fearful that the Jerries would tumble their escape plot. There were some near misses, but the German guards were fooled again and again. They didn't find out what had been happening until one of the escaping prisoners was caught. 'Albert' was subsequently put on show in a war museum in Germany but I believe he was destroyed during one of our air-raids on Berlin.

John made another 'Albert' for the film and I must say he looked uncannily real. In the fictional version of this real-life story, Worsley was called Lieutenant Geoffrey Ainsworth and the part was played by Anthony Steel. It was an all-male cast, which was taking quite a chance at the box-office, but the film was warmly received by the critics and did extremely well. In the matter of service rank I took quite a step up—from army corporal in *The Captive Heart* to naval captain in *Albert R.N.*

Guy Middleton was in both films and introduced a spot of light comedy in what was basically a sombre story. Once again Robert Beatty was with me plus Michael Balfour, Eddie Byrne, Frederick Valk, Anton Diffring, Paul Carpenter and Peter Jones.

Paul Carpenter was a Canadian who had been a professional ice-hockey player and war correspondent before he joined Ted Heath's band and became one of Britain's favourite singers alongside Denis Lotis. It is interesting to recall that Jack Parnell —now often espied in the background of musical shows equipped with headphones and conducting an orchestra—was Ted Heath's young drummer. Paul became extremely popular and did a lot of broadcasting before he was finally attracted by offers from film producers here and in America.

Sadly, his private life began to fall apart. He and fellow Canadian Bonar Colleano were great buddies and when Bonar was killed in a car crash in 1958, Paul went to pieces. But greatly to his credit he fought back and rebuilt his career. He was not too proud to accept minor parts in provincial stage shows but by the end of 1960 was again doing well, particularly in television. He was without question an actor with talent to spare.

In 1964 he turned down a part in *Goldfinger*, the James Bond film, to appear in a play called *The First Fish* which was due to open at the Savoy Theatre. This proved to be a strange and cruel twist of fate. In spite of his earlier stage successes, Paul had never starred in a West End play and understandably looked upon *The First Fish* as a potential break. But it wasn't to be. He went to his dressing room to rest after rehearsal on June 12th—and three hours later was found lying dead on a settee. He had only recently recovered from injuries received in a car accident, but appeared to be in good health and his sudden death was a great shock to his many friends.

Paul was buried only a few yards away from the grave of his old pal, Bonar, at Chiswick.

Peter Jones has come a long way since *Albert R.N.*, in which he had quite a small part. He is, in fact, a shining example of an early comic who has developed into a complete all-rounder. He's been on radio and television with Peter Ustinov in a clever show called *In All Directions*, done very well on the legitimate stage, and has written several plays. His fans have multiplied as the result of his appearances in his own T.V. series and also in *The Rag Trade*, *Beggar my Neighbour*, *Mr Digby Darling* and *Kindly Leave the Kerb*.

Few people know that Peter is keen on yoga and enjoys five minutes' deep relaxation before every performance. I'm told this has created a good deal of alarm when people have discovered him flat out in his dressing room. On more than one occasion callers feared that he was dead.

Not long ago, Peter was a guest on the *Reg Varney Comedy Hour*—Reg being another comedian who did splendidly in *The Rag Trade*. I've known Reg for many years and recall his appearance at the Lido, Cliftonville, a long time ago. I was so impressed when I saw his act there that I went back-stage to offer him my congratulations. I was quite bewildered when he said dejectedly, 'Oh, Jack, I don't know, I shan't get anywhere.'

I talked to him as I had talked to Tony Hancock. 'Give yourself a chance,' I said. 'You've plenty of wonderful talent. Don't talk like that. . . .' He declined to be comforted. Then he was given a spot in *The Rag Trade* and has never looked back. Audiences have long acclaimed him as a comedian but I think many people were surprised by his own comedy hour when he illustrated his fantastic technique as a pianist and first-rate accordionist. He could earn a damned good living that way.

There are very few occasions when members of the theatrical profession can afford to take a voluntary holiday and turn away work. I've heard many country and seaside publicans say, when coining it in the summer, 'I may be taking it now but it will be a long winter.' The same applies to actors except that their slack period is hardly seasonal and can come at any time. So, when the work is there only a fool fails to grab it. It was like that for me when *Albert R.N.* was completed. I went straight into *Bang! You're Dead* and *Forbidden Cargo*—with exactly two hours' break between finishing the first and starting the second. I left Shepperton Studios at around 5 p.m. one November day in 1953, after shooting the final scenes of *Bang! You're Dead,* and by 7.15 that evening I was at Victoria Station and already at work on *Forbidden Cargo* until 4 a.m. the next day.

I played very different parts in the two films. In the first, the story of a small boy who accidentally kills a man, I was cast as the lad's father. This was rather a grim picture although realistic at the time. It was set in post-war rural England where abandoned Nissen huts were taken over by squatters, and nobody seemed to care what happened to the kids. Gordon

Harker had a good part as a pub landlord and the cast included Derek Farr and Michael Medwin.

Forbidden Cargo was an exciting yarn about drug smugglers who were thwarted by Customs officers, in the persons of Nigel Patrick and myself, assisted by a daffy bird-watcher, Joyce Grenfell. Terence Morgan, who had recently returned from Rome where he had been starring in a film with the voluptuous Hedy Lamarr, was the villain-in-chief. The leading lady was Joan Collins, who took part in the early shooting, but, for some reason I can't recall, left the cast and was replaced by Elizabeth Sellars.

At the time Nigel's son was about two and I remember buying him a tiny armchair of which he was very proud. He certainly won't fit it now because he must be the thick end of twenty-two.

While making this picture I became slightly involved in a real-life crime. Thieves forced a window at Pinewood Studios, where the film was made, and blew open the office safe containing pay packets worth £10,000. They got away with the lot. At the time, Dirk Bogarde, Jack Hawkins, Glynis Johns, Kenneth More, Donald Sinden and Donald Houston were all working at the studios on different film sets and we all teamed up to try and assist the C.I.D. I suspect we were more of a hindrance than a help but the national newspapers got a bit of fun out of our amateur sleuthing.

On November 12th, 1953, I had the honour to appear in the Royal Variety performance at the London Coliseum in aid of the Variety Artistes Benevolent Fund. It was also the year of the Coronation and was attended by the then young Queen Elizabeth, the Duke of Edinburgh, Princess Margaret and the Duchess of Kent. Now, I would challenge any performer to deny that on an occasion like this or even on a first appearance in a big West End theatre, he or she doesn't feel nervous. I suffered agonising misgivings and not the least of my problems on that night was what should I do for the audience.

Quite a few years had elapsed since I had made my first

appearance at the London Palladium—in a Sunday concert a few weeks before we were due to open there with *Garrison Theatre.* On that occasion, I had concentrated upon perfecting the solo act I had been doing for some time and had then thrown in a few excerpts that had been made famous by the *Garrison Theatre* radio show like, 'Mind my Bike', and the funny occupation—a 'Bunger up o' Rat 'oles'. The radio show was then going great guns and consequently I was accorded a terrific reception. When I had finished my act I was called back again and again and George Black, the producer, was delighted.

But by the time the Royal night came on this occasion I had done so many different things in the theatre that I was bedevilled by doubt in trying to decide what act would be the most appropriate. I had, as it were, become a man of many parts and I wondered which part the audience would like me to play. It was a pity that I couldn't put the question to them but I had to make the decision myself and I believe that on the night I made the wrong one.

I had wrestled with the problem many nights into the small hours. Should I put on a working man's ill-fitting suit and be Joe Huggett—*Meet the Huggetts* had been launched on radio earlier that year and I then possessed the Joe Huggett image—or should I wear a conventional dinner jacket and be myself, filling the eight or ten allotted minutes with running tales of quaint occupations. I chose the last named and did a monologue about an old gardener, also an impression of Maurice Chevalier. I realised too late that I would have come off much better by chatting up the audience as Joe Huggett!

It was in no way a good night for me. I remember there were the usual back-stage anxieties—'What are they like?'—'Are they going to be stuffy?' Such an audience is not easy to win over. The people have paid an awful lot of money for their seats and sometimes feel they are not required to applaud. When they do it is more of a polite acknowledgement than a spontaneous response and this can be most disconcerting to the artistes. Actually, they weren't too bad that night and I had a fairly good reception, but I was not happy my about act and was very nervous.

The circumstances were unfavourable because I had to work to a front cloth and would rather have presented my act as I usually did, with a grand piano on the stage with Bobby Alderson seated there. He carries all my music in his head, which makes for smooth collaboration. I was also put off by scenery being moved behind the drop curtain. The wings were so close that I had to squeeze on to the stage and, as a consequence, the brand new dinner-suit I was wearing was smudged all down the back.

These irritations may appear trivial, but they can throw you when you are under a lot of tension. But I have never made any excuses for my act. I made a big mistake and chose the wrong thing. The terrible realisation hit me when I was halfway through my performance. I learned a lesson—what goes down well with a music-hall audience is not necessarily the right material for a Royal Command performance.

I well recall some of the other stars of that night—a formidable collection of talent—Jimmy Edwards, Tommy Cooper, Alfred Marks, Eve Boswell, Edmund Hockridge, Lizbeth Webb, Anne Shelton and Vivian Blaine, the American actress of several musicals, including *Pal Joey*. But the one who impressed me most was Max Bygraves, who although many years my junior, had become, because of his innumerable appearances, the 'daddy' of Royal Command shows.

Max is one of the most popular chaps in show business and seems to have a magic touch—or perhaps I should say the sensitive touch of a surgeon. He 'feels' an audience and hits them in the right place at precisely the right moment and with the right material. Today he sings ordinary songs for ordinary people, those that people can whistle—and they stand the test of time.

Having been, by my own standards, a bit of a flop at the 1953 show, I was delighted when I was again invited to take part in another Royal Variety show in 1956. I made up my mind to perfect an act that would go over in a big way but the planning and rehearsing all of us were engaged in was wrecked by the Suez crisis—the show was abruptly cancelled.

In addition to being chosen for two Command performances, I have taken part several times in the stage entertainment that is a feature of the Royal Command film premières at which it is traditional for members of the Royal Family present to receive the artists who have taken part.

I recall a notable occasion when Princess Elizabeth, as she then was, and the Duke of Edinburgh fulfilled this duty. It was in the heyday of the Huggett pictures but on the night in question I was not, of course, wearing my 'Huggett' suit but correctly attired in full dress—white tie, tails and white waistcoat. Princess Elizabeth addressed a few words to me and I was still standing to attention when the Duke approached. He looked at me very hard for perhaps a second or two and then, with a positive twinkle in his eye, remarked. 'You don't look a bit like Joe Huggett to me!'

King George VI, Queen Elizabeth and the two princesses attended the 1950 film showing, which was really a star-studded affair. The film chosen for the occasion was *The Mudlark* in which Ted Ray's son, Andrew, then aged twelve, played the title role.

More than thirty British and American actors took part in the stage show including James Stewart, who was compere, John Mills, Tyrone Power and Montgomery Clift. The trio sang a Noël Coward number called 'Three Juvenile Delinquents', and ageless, ever-glamorous Marlene Dietrich sang 'Lili Marlene'.

It was an evening I thoroughly enjoyed. Wearing a white satin dress-suit and white topper, I was one of a male sextet who sang 'Tell Me Pretty Maiden' from the old musical comedy *Floradora.* David Farrar was asked to take part in this number but apparently was averse to appearing in white satin and declined the invitation. The final male line-up was Jack Hawkins, Robert Beatty, John McCallum, Richard Todd, Michael Wilding and myself and we were partnered by Margaret Lockwood, Googie Withers, Valeri Hobson, Margaret Leighton, Glynis Johns and Bebe Daniels.

There was something ominously prophetic about a revue sketch presented at the 1951 Royal Film Show. It was called *The World Film Crisis* and was supposed to foreshadow in a comic way the effect of television on the film industry. Richard Attenborough pushed a pram with a gramophone, Hermione Baddeley appeared as a flower seller, and Zachary Scott, Phyllis Calvert and myself sat on a park bench trying to make a living by selling hot chestnuts and balloons. It all seemed rather a lark at the time, but it isn't so funny now when one reflects upon the number of cinemas that have been sold, demolished or converted to bingo halls during the past twenty years!

The all-day rehearsal for the show took place in a room above a cinema in Tottenham Court Road. It was a very jolly occasion, with Jane Russell in slacks and a fur coat playing the piano for an informal sing-song which wound up the proceedings. The late Margaret Rutherford was present, as were Burt Lancaster, Fred McMurray, Jean Kent, Valerie Hobson and many others. They were all top names in the movie world but they had mucked in together to help the Cinematograph Trade Benevolent Fund—the primary object of the Royal Command film shows. It was a day that reminded me of those happy and comradely times that I had shared with the Fol-de-Rols all those years ago.

CHAPTER 11

Sunday Freedom Association

THE RATE of production of movies today is very slow compared with the first fifteen years of the post-war period. The reduction in demand has, of course, been dictated by the popularity of televiewing.

Looking back, it seems quite phenomenal that during the nine years prior to 1954 I made no less than twenty-five pictures, a figure that takes no account of the activities of other players. As I mentioned earlier, the salary figures on our contracts did not read exactly like telephone numbers, but the industry was healthy, the audiences appreciative and we were all making a comfortable living.

Twenty-five films, almost three a year, plus stage appearances, represented a considerable working schedule and therefore I wasn't altogether sorry to find myself free of immediate studio commitments after completing *Forbidden Cargo*. Although I didn't realise it at the time, fewer films were to come my way and my career was to take a different turn within the next twelve months.

In other ways, 1954 was a busy year of mixed interests and activities. I was in my second season with the Huggetts on radio and I was doing a lot more radio and television work. In February, I worked with the late Vic Oliver in the B.B.C.'s *Variety Playhouse* and in April made a television appearance in *This is Show Business*.

Elsewhere I gave a number of concerts and charity shows, but much of my time was absorbed in a cause very close to my heart —the Sunday Freedom Association, which had (and still has) as its primary object, the removal of anomalies in the law as they affect Sabbath activities in this country.

The association was formed in 1947 after the English Table Tennis Association was obliged to cancel its annual South of England championships at Hastings because of the intervention of the Lord's Day Observance Society. Kenneth Day, who was Hastings entertainments manager, was so disgusted by the Society's action, that he organised a public protest meeting which was attended by representatives of British Actors' Equity, the Variety Artistes' Federation, the Concert Artistes' Association, the Musicians' Union and other show business and sporting organisations. 'Misery' Martin, the general secretary of the Lord's Day Observance Society, was also present and demonstrated the absolute inflexibility of his views by walking from London to Hastings to avoid using public transport on a Sunday!

At this meeting, the Sunday Freedom Association was born, to secure the repeal of the Sunday Observance Acts of the 17th and 18th centuries and the Sunday Entertainments Act, 1932. This act permits performances of musical entertainment on Sundays, the term being defined as 'a concert or similar entertainment consisting of the performance of music with or without singing or recitation'. It is, of course, somewhat ambiguous but it is generally interpreted to mean that comedy acts, cross-talk, props, costumes and make-up are forbidden.

Unhappily, Kenneth Day died within weeks of the formation of the association and Mr. William Sensier, of Worcester Park, Surrey, took his place as general secretary. I became president and we both retain these positions today, although we are conscious of the fact that we have not made as much progress as we had hoped in getting rid of these ludicrous laws.

Mr. John Parker, M.P. for Dagenham, joined our cause as Parliamentary adviser and we also had the support of Peter Kirk, M.P. for Thanet, and Denis Howell, M.P. for Birmingham. We have held a number of meetings in the House of Commons and I became quite a familiar figure in the House—but only in the central Lobby!

Despite opposition from other Members, our big chance finally arrived. In 1953 John Parker was fortunate enough to draw a Private Members' Bill and we were pitched in at the deep end. The main purpose of this Bill was to remove many of the restrictions upon personal freedom on Sundays and we went all out to whip up the support we hoped would bring us victory.

Bill Sensier and I were interviewed by Anthony Wedgwood Benn in a programme called *Speaking Personally* which was televised live, and Bill also took part in a number of *Taking Stock* programmes on radio.

The late Gilbert Harding gave us a lot of support and as a result of his column in one of the Sunday newspapers we recruited many new members. Bill and I were convinced that the Church of England did not see eye to eye with the Lord's Day Observance Society and in an endeavour to further strengthen our campaign, I wrote to Dr Fisher, then Archbishop of Canterbury, asking if he would grant me an interview. He agreed and displayed sympathy with our efforts, as will be seen in the following extract from a letter he later sent to me: 'I can make the position of the Church quite clear. There is a general agreement that the present legislation is not only completely out of date but in many respects ridiculous and the cause of offence. More than once, responsible bodies of the Church have urged that the Government should take in hand a modernisation of this legislation.'

In spite of all our efforts, John Parker's Bill was defeated by twenty votes and an amendment calling for a Royal Commission to examine the entire matter failed by eight votes. We were disappointed at this setback but determined as ever to carry on with our campaign, so I was glad to have the break from filming which allowed me to give more time to this in 1954.

In March that year we sponsored a Sunday concert at Kilburn which was designed to show just how absurd were the existing laws. Nan Kenway and Douglas Young appeared together but didn't speak to each other because to do so would have been a contravention of the law. Other artistes cracked their customary jokes but strung them together to form a 'recitation' which came within the law. I did my Chevalier impersonation—minus a straw hat!

The business of having to appear without the hat struck me as the height of stupidity. Some years before, I had actually been wearing the hat as I strolled along the beach at Llandudno one Sunday, yet I had to remove it to appear on stage that evening because it was classified as 'costume'.

On another occasion, I was doing the Chevalier piece and decided to wear the hat—although I was appearing at a Sunday concert. During my act I noticed three fellows sitting in the front row of the audience busily taking notes and after the show they came backstage to see me.

'You were wearing a straw hat,' said one accusingly.

'I know I was.'

'But you can't do that—it's against the law.'

I looked him straight in the eyes and said, 'I arrived at the theatre wearing the hat and I continued to wear it on the stage. I could have worn a Red Indian head-dress during my act if I'd been wearing it when I arrived here. I can, in fact, appear in anything, provided I was wearing it before I entered the theatre and that it was my normal dress. How do you know what I usually wear?'

The trio departed in some confusion.

In the days when I was appearing in *Garrison Theatre* I wore my usual battledress to give a Sunday show and the Lord's Day Observance Soviety were after me again. I was compelled to change into civilian clothes, otherwise they could have forced the manager to ring down the curtain on the whole production.

In 1952, when I was in *The Blue Lamp* on stage at Blackpool, I wanted to do a Sunday performance in aid of the Lynton and Lynmouth Flood Disaster Fund. There were sixteen or seventeen shows running in Blackpool at that time and each company was anxious to give their services free for this worthy cause. I went to see the Chief Constable to explain the situation and to try and pave the way for all of us to go on.

With great reluctance he shook his head and said, 'I'm sorry, but you just can't do it. If you do, you will be breaking the law.'

He was right and he had no choice in the matter but it was nonetheless a deplorable dilemma. We could have raised a lot of money for those poor people who had lost so much when the River Lyn changed its course after torrential rain and brought disaster to a quiet corner of Devonshire.

I remember another incident that infuriated me. I was booked to do a Sunday show in the Midlands to raise money for war-wounded sailors. The event had been well publicised, but when I arrived at the theatre for the band call in the afternoon, the manager warned me not to expect a very good house. When I asked him why, he told me that the Lord's Day Observance supporters had spread the rumour that I would not be appearing because I was not allowed to work on Sundays.

As soon as I walked on to the stage I could see that the manager's pessimism was justified, the theatre was only half full. Mid-way in my act, I stopped the orchestra, explained to the audience what had happened, and appealed to those who could afford it to contribute something over and above the admission price. There was a great response and we raised a sizeable sum which compensated for the money lost on unsold seats.

Apart from any other consideration, there is no rhyme or reason to these silly Sunday entertainment laws. At charity cricket matches, for instance, no admission charge may be made—but it's O.K. to collect money for the deckchairs. I believe I am right in stating too that although a charity darts match is allowed to take place on the Sabbath, a charity snooker tournament is forbidden.

It's even more idiotic in the world of stage entertainment. A ventriloquist may do his act—but mustn't use his dummy! So how does he do his act? My sisters Elsie and Doris may appear on the stage—provided they wear their everyday dresses, stand eight feet apart and don't speak to each other!

I regret that our Sunday Freedom Association has not been able to do more. These archaic laws are still on the Statute Book although there are loopholes for those sufficiently cunning to find and exploit them.

In retrospect, 1954 was a very mixed year—both in the work I did and the degree of success I achieved. *The Huggetts* was undoubtedly a popular series and attracted many more listeners during its second season but my summer season at Blackpool's Grand Theatre in Jack Hylton's stage presentation of the radio serial, *The Archers*, was frankly disappointing. Lots of people thought that because it was such a great success on the radio—and still is, as we all know—it would be just as popular on stage. It didn't happen that way at all and it certainly didn't catch on in the way *The Blue Lamp* had done at the same resort two years' earlier. Perhaps it wasn't right for Lancashire audiences. I don't know but I think we only just managed to break even financially.

I played Dan Archer and Joyce Barbour took the part of my wife. Peter Byrne, who was soon to start his long partnership with me in *Dixon*, was our son Philip, and that great character actor, Charlie Victor, played old Walter Gabriel.

I remember one night when Charlie, who was in one scene supposed to run out of the back door, slipped and fell flat on his back. I was so concerned that I just shouted, 'Oh Charlie!' It sounded a bit silly in the middle of the Archers.

Charlie, in the tradition of the grand old trouper, remained completely unflustered and ad libbed in his Walter Gabriel voice, 'It's all right boy, I'll get out of this. . . .'

Kay Callard, a young Canadian actress, had a part in this play and was called upon to strip to her panties and bra after supposedly being caught in a rainstorm. Of course, it wouldn't have been quite proper in those days for young Phil Archer to have seen Kay in her undies and he remained primly out of sight! Even so, it was all considered to be rather daring. How times have changed! It is extremely difficult to put before an audience a show based on a long-running radio series. Listeners create for themselves their own images of the characters who have become familiar to them, but when they supposedly appear on the stage in the flesh, likely as not, the show becomes depressingly unrealistic to the audience.

Many people will remember Dorothy Summers as the char-lady in *ITMA* and her famous catch-phrase, 'Can I do you now, sir?' Dorothy went on to the halls wearing a smart frock and her act didn't quite come off. Audiences had expected to see her with a bucket, mop and a man's cap. It shows how essential it is that the radio character remains unchanged in a performance before an audience. I remember sharing a bill in Aberdeen for three weeks with Harry Gordon, a wonderful Scottish comedian who could always pack them in over the border. His popularity led to a booking at the London Palladium.

During the years he had appeared on the halls in Scotland, he had always worn a kilt, but for his London show he discarded it in favour of a dinner jacket. 'That,' he admitted, 'was a mistake.' His reception from the public lacked the warmth that he would have been given had he appeared for what he was—a full-blooded Scottish artist.

Albert Burdon was a gifted knock-about comedian who built up a tremendous following in northern towns and cities in shows such as *The League of Notions* and *On the Dole*. He wore a ridiculous stuck-on ginger moustache and sometimes a woolly tam-o'-shanter. I remember one of his sketches called 'The Lightning Shave' in which he played the part of a non-stop barber, making the sparks fly from a leather strop as he sharpened the razor and then covered the customer with soap-suds in the best slapstick tradition. I saw his *League of Notions* show three times in one week and witnessed an incident I have never seen before or since. A man sitting in the stalls just in front of me laughed so much that he broke a blood vessel and had to be carried from the theatre. I'd heard about making people laugh fit to bust, but this was ridiculous. Eventually C. B. Cochran saw Albert and decided to launch him in the West End. On all known form he should have been a riot, but he wasn't—merely because they took away his moustache and tam-o'-shanter and put him in a dinner jacket. He had a tremendous battle trying to raise a laugh. Albert did all right later but never seemed to reach the peak of comedy he achieved in *League of Notions*. I have always felt that he never received a fair crack of the whip. It was a pity because he was such a clever and inventive comic.

I almost suffered the same fate. In the early days of *Garrison Theatre* on the stage I was provided with a brand new Rudge Whitworth bicycle and an immaculate uniform. I was horrified. The two things would have made me a cardboard character. Who would have believed that I was radio's common Cockney soldier 'minding my bike'? I came up with a grubby uniform, a real bone-shaker of a bike, shoved my cap on the back of my head and cycled down the gangway of the auditorium. George Black, who was standing at the back of the stalls as I approached, muttered, 'What the hell is he playing at?' But I knew I was right. I was the character the audience expected to see.

Apart from the disappointment at the near-flop of *The Archers*, I also found the show rather tiring. We were doing two performances nightly, six nights a week, and on Sundays I had to travel to London to record the next episode of *The Huggetts*. This meant joining the 3.20 a.m. London train at Wigan every Sunday and travelling back to Blackpool early each Monday morning. I remember that once, during a twenty-minute break in *The Huggetts*, I did an Anthony Newley and fell asleep on the studio floor!

Perhaps I could have coped better with the physical strain if

The Archers had been more successful. Few people outside of the theatrical profession can appreciate how an actor feels if he is playing in a show which he knows is not going down with the audience as it should.

With a one-night show, if things do not go quite right, one is very conscious of it at the time, but gradually the memory fades because the next engagement is just around the corner and probably the next night, if all goes well, you are on top of the world again.

It so happened that during that year, Mollie and I opened a health food shop, but the event was in no way connected with the Blackpool situation. The venture was triggered off by a meeting I had had the previous year with a nature-cure practitioner.

In the early part of 1953, just before I made *Albert R.N.*, I developed a painful condition in my feet which I thought was probably gout. I was extremely worried when it showed no signs of improving because I had already signed a film contract and was fully committed. It certainly would not have done to have had a naval officer hobbling around the prison camp like an old man. Mollie heard about the practitioner, whose name was Spenceley, and I went to see him.

He told me immediately that I was well overweight and although I was hardly conscious of the fact, I couldn't disagree. I was about sixteen stones and even for a man of my height it was obvious that I was carrying far too many pounds —or stones!

'I'll put you on a fast,' said Spenceley. He said fast and not diet and that was exactly what he meant. He sent me home to bed and told me I wasn't to eat anything. Water provided me with my only sustenance for two whole weeks. It had to work. I lost two stones and felt really marvellous.

Spenceley visited me twice a day and when I had achieved the weight loss he allowed me to get up and walk around the garden at my Kent home. He warned me that I would feel weak, but in fact, and much to my surprise, I didn't.

I was put on a light diet and three days later was able to drive myself to London to be fitted for my naval uniform for the film. When it was released, several critics remarked upon the new slim Warner—vastly different from the one in *The Final Test* and *The Square Ring*.

Apart from the loss of body weight, I became much thinner in the face, making me look a good deal younger. My foot trouble had completely vanished.

Mr Spenceley, who had surgeries in Ramsgate and Canterbury, told us that there was a need for a health food shop in the cathedral city, and it occurred to us that we might open one there. Apart from our interest in health foods we realised it was not a bad idea for anyone to have a second string to his bow. As events turned out this wasn't really necessary but at the time I was by no means certain of what the future had in store for me.

The following year we found a tiny shop near King's School, Canterbury. We opened in May, 1954. Business was so good that not long afterwards we were forced to move to bigger premises. Luckily we were able to find a first-class manageress and a van driver. Mollie spent a lot of time at the shop herself and the business continued to prosper over the next few years. In 1961 the manageress decided to move on and we began to have doubts of being able to replace her with someone equally efficient and trustworthy. Mollie, too, was beginning to feel the strain of overseeing the business and coping with my theatrical affairs, so we were forced, reluctantly, to sell.

As a result of Mr. Spenceley's treatment, and our experiences with health food, Mollie and I became very diet conscious and much more fussy about the food we ate. I soon came to the conclusion that I worked much better by eating moderately and that after a long day's work I just could not go home to a big meal. I know many people in the profession who nightly eat enormous meals after the show is over, having eaten very little, if anything, during the day. They suffer for it afterwards.

Animals can teach us a lot when it comes to natural behaviour. If a cat or a dog is off-colour it automatically rejects food and sleeps. It will only return to feed when its condition improves. I find that I'm much more mentally alert if I eat moderately and there is so much truth in the old adage that one should eat to live and not live to eat.

Since my fast, I've always tried to keep my weight to reasonable proportions. If I don't I soon face trouble with the leg that has given me problems ever since filming *Train of Events*.

It is relatively easy for me to exercise this type of self-discipline because Mollie follows a similar regimen. If we attend a public dinner of say five or even six courses, we restore the balance on the following day by eating nothing but fruit and we find this keeps us in pretty good shape.

We eat only wholemeal bread when we are at home and instead of taking white sugar in our tea and coffee we use honey. We avoid fried foods and supplement our diet with as much organically grown food as possible. Generally we prefer grilled food plus plenty of salads, vegetables and fruit.

When I was a small boy, my mother used to cook some wonderful meals for us—roast beef, boiled mutton and caper sauce, boiled pork and pease pudding. Excellent food for growing children burning calories like a furnace burns coke every minute of the day, but I think as the years roll by moderation becomes more important than ever, especially if opportunities for exercise become fewer or if one is physically precluded from taking part.

Towards the end of the mixed year of 1954, I was asked if I would like to do a television series based on the character of George Dixon, the copper who had been killed in *The Blue Lamp*. Ted (now Lord) Willis, who had written the script for the film, had resuscitated Dixon and made him the central character in a number of stories about the man-on-the-beat. The series was to be called *Dixon of Dock Green*, in which I resumed my film role, and was scheduled to run for six weeks. Ronnie Waldman, then in charge of light entertainment at the

B.B.C. was delighted at the idea and once I had read the wonderful scripts I became equally enthusiastic.

I told the Rank Organisation that I wanted to be released from my contract and, as I had signed for seven years and remained for nine, no real objection to my request could be raised. But they weren't all that keen about my departure when I told them of my television engagement because the 'box' was very much resented by the movie industry. Television was not new to me. I had made my first T.V. appearance in 1935.

In fact, I made two more films before starting on the *Dixon* series. The first, for Hammer Films, was *The Quatermass Experiment*, the only X film with which I was ever associated and it was given the rating because in those days it was regarded as being rather horrific. Based upon the television serial of the same title it was a somewhat ahead-of-its-time story, about a manned space rocket and what happened to the sole survivor of the experiment. Hollywood's Brian Donlevy was Quatermass and I played the police chief in charge of the civilian end of the affair.

The second film, of which I am able to recall only the barest details, was entitled *Now and Forever* and was directed by Mario Zampi. We were on location in the Lake District in June, 1955, and I remember Mollie was able to join me and share a working holiday in that lovely part of the country. I played the father of Janette Scott, an unhappy schoolgirl who eloped with her boyfriend. Their plan to marry in Scotland was thwarted when their car crashed over a precipice at Hardknott.

By the time *The Quartermass Experiment* had been released in the summer of 1955, I had completed the first six episodes of *Dixon* and the series had been launched on television. People who had seen the film and were now watching the T.V. series must have been amused by my rapid 'promotion'—from Dixon, the bobby on the beat, to a top ranking detective—in a matter of days!

CHAPTER 12

Carve her Name with Pride

THE FIRST production of *Dixon of Dock Green* was televised on July 1st, 1955, and was simply the story of an ordinary copper on the beat. The interest it created not only confirmed the view that a series could easily be sustained but that the capture of a mass audience was well on the cards. Very few people, it seemed, had ever spared a thought for the policeman as an individual whose problems differed very slightly, if at all, from those of the rest of the community. It was necessary, therefore, to present him as a human character with a normal, warm, family background. George Dixon was thus introduced as a widower and father-figure sharing his domestic life with Mary, his daughter, and to a certain extent with Andy Crawford, a young constable who was their lodger and, ultimately, George's son-in-law.

Fan mail quickly made it obvious that the people in the new series had become as real—especially members of the Dixon family—as the characters in *Mrs Dale's Diary*, *The Archers* and *Coronation Street* were to their listeners and viewers.

It is, of course, impossible not to take cognisance of the sociological changes in moods and manners that occur over the years and, as a police series, the advent of violence, new forms of organised crime and the so-called sexual freedoms, compelled us to revise the programme's early concept. It meant that the so-called 'cosy' relationships in the family would have to go and action would have to be concentrated upon the criminal content of the stories if we were to compete successfully with new and tough crime series, many of them American, then appearing on both channels.

I'm an actor and not paid to be an arbiter of public taste—nor do I have access to market research investigations which are supposed to reflect public tastes. But we are now in our nineteenth year of *Dixon* with a viewing figure of fifteen millions and I still have fans who ask me why 'family' matters no longer figure in any of our stories. Without doubt, the demand for light-hearted domestic comedy series—mentioned earlier in the book—does seem to show that the public is ready to watch or listen to something a little more gentle. Of course, I could be awfully wrong!

Viewers will recall that Arthur Rigby, who was the station sergeant in *The Blue Lamp*, had the same role in the television series for nearly ten years. He then left and the part was taken over by Duncan Lamont for a single series. When Duncan departed because of other commitments, I received 'promotion'. Sadly, Arthur died.

As Andy Crawford, Peter Byrne has given and still gives me magnificent support—nowadays as the detective-inspector. We are father and son-in-law on the box, but away from the studios I often feel we are almost like father and son in real life.

Peter has a terrific sense of humour and also a great ability to imitate sounds and impersonate people. Sometimes when we have had a river scene in *Dixon*, his sound of a ship's siren has momentarily fooled us. Everyone has an occasional off-day, but when I hit a flat period Peter's presence is better than any tonic. Most people tend to identify him exclusively with the part of Andy Crawford but he is actually a most versatile actor well known on the West End stage. Two of his most successful appearances were in *Boeing Boeing* and *There's a Girl in my Soup*. Both plays ran for a long time.

Probably few people will remember that the part of my daughter in the first six series of *Dixon* was played by Billie Whitelaw who later rocketed to fame. Her part was taken over by Jeanette Hutchinson, who stayed with us for about ten years until she was gently eased out to care for her 'children' in the 'home' she shares with 'Andy'.

The initial success of the first six *Dixon* parts prompted producer Ronnie Waldman to ask Ted Willis for twelve more scripts.

The B.B.C wanted me to start the second series at the beginning of 1956, but I was still on the road with *Hippo Dancing* and was also committed to making another movie entitled *Home and Away* which, like *Easy Money*, made nine years earlier, was about a big win on the football pools. I played the part of a power-station foreman living in a suburban villa, and once again Kathleen Harrison appeared as my wife. I'm sure that some people became quite convinced that Kathleen and I were actually husband and wife in real life because we were paired so often.

Charlie Victor, who had been with me in the stage version of *The Archers*, had a major part in *Home and Away* with Thora Hird as his wife. Other familiar players of the period in the film were Sam Kydd, Janette Scott and Harry Fowler.

I am one of the millions who regularly fill in a football coupon each week during the English soccer season. I confess to knowing almost as little about the game as I know about the finer points of cricket, but I enjoy the anticipation each Saturday brings although, alas, it has not resulted in any rich reward. Perhaps that isn't surprising because I place my crosses for ten draws against the names of towns and cities in whose music-halls I have played over the past forty years. I cannot claim my system is particularly scientific but it's marginally more interesting than just blindly sticking a pin in the paper. I have more than over-subscribed to my solitary win of forty-four pounds! Like the fisherman who can't forget about the big one that just got away, I can only state that one more correct draw on that occasion would have netted me a packet. But that's the stuff of which dreams are made!

After *Home and Away* I returned to the television studios for the second *Dixon* series in August, 1956—when the highlight for many viewers was Mary's 'wedding' to Andy—and I exchanged my constable's uniform for a smart suit complete with carnation. Just two years later I was one of the guests at the real-life wedding of Jeanette Hutchinson—my 'daughter' Mary at Dock Green—when she married musician Al Baum at a ceremony watched with interest by her T.V. 'husband', Peter Byrne. My, it does sometimes sound confusing!

We had reached the fifth series of *Dixon* by September, 1958, and had achieved a viewing public of fourteen million but in the interim, I managed to fulfil a role in *Carve her Name with Pride*. I truly believe that this was one of the finest—if not the finest—film in which I have ever appeared.

It was adapted from the true story of Violette Szabo, a modest young English girl who lived in Brixton and worked behind a counter at Woolworths, until she met and married a Free French Army officer during the last war. Two years later he was killed at El Alamein and Violette was invited to serve as a British agent behind enemy lines. She was parachuted into France and carried out some chilling exploits with the Resistance Group before being arrested and tortured. She was then removed to Ravensbrück and finally shot by the Germans. Violette died heroically without disclosing the names of her comrades or revealing the secret of the touching little poem which was the key to the code used to send her messages back to London. She was posthumously awarded the George Cross.

The part of Violette was most tenderly portrayed by Virginia McKenna, who brought to life the character of a quiet, unassuming shop girl whose courage could not be broken. Produced by Danny Angel and directed by Lewis Gilbert, the film was splendidly presented and so moving that it brought tears to the eyes of many cinemagoers.

I played the part of Violette's father, and a scene I recall vividly was one in which I rebuked her for staying out late at night, neglecting her job and—as I thought—fooling around. She refused to defend herself, but as she hurried upstairs to bed she took a handkerchief out of her pocket, and in doing so dropped something on the floor. I recognised it as a badge given to special parachute agents. I followed Violette to her room and let her know that I was aware what she was up to. Quite simply she said that I was not supposed to know and added, 'Don't tell Mother.' The scene was played in a low key and the dialogue pared to a brief exchange, but I shall always remember it as one of the most meaningful I have ever played.

Towards the end of the picture there is a sequence in which I visited Buckingham Palace with Violette's little daughter, who is to receive the George Cross on behalf of a mother she is too young to remember. Clearly we could not ask King George VI to make the award, as he had done in real life, and the problem as to who should represent the King was solved by Paul Schofield. He had played Violette's commanding officer and it is his arm in Admiral's tunic that is seen coming forward to pin the medal on to the child's coat.

There has been a revival of public interest recently in the heroic story of Violette Szabo. The code poem, 'The Love That I Have', was recited by Virginia McKenna on the B.B.C.'s Pete Murray record programme *Open House* in February, 1974, and so many listeners requested a copy of the words that Virginia recorded the poem to a choral background. The poem runs:

The life that I have
Is all that I have,
And the life that I have
Is yours.
The love that I have
Of the life that I have
Is yours and yours and yours.

A sleep I shall have,
A rest I shall have,
Yet death will be but a pause;
For the peace of my years
In the long green grass
Will be yours and yours and yours.

It has now been revealed that the author of the poem was Leo Marks, who during the war was Codemaster with Special Operations Executive Group and is now a scriptwriter. Mr. Marks explained that he had to use original poems to prevent the Germans cracking the code. He had previously refused permission for his authorship to be divulged but changed his mind when a little boy with only a few weeks to live wrote to the B.B.C. to ask about Violette and the poem.

The tenuous connection between the tragedy of Violette's torture and death and the fate of a little boy, who became interested in the story of her wartime exploits, is touched with unbearable melancholy illuminated by an act of great kindness. Mr. Marks sent the child a chess set which had been given to him by Violette during her training as a British agent.

The part of Violette was particularly suited to Virginia McKenna's talents. She is an actress who has made some truly splendid films, including *A Town Like Alice* and *Born Free*, in which she spent over a year on location in Africa in the role of Joy Adamson, the woman who raised a wild lioness as a pet. Virginia is a naturally gentle and sympathetic person and, to that extent, was able to be herself in the films I have mentioned, but she is an exceptionally versatile actress and has appeared in a variety of roles—the naughty Daisy, Countess of Warwick, in *The Edwardians* on B.B.C. 2, as the wife of a Prime Minister in *The Beheading* on the West End stage, as the mother of the eccentric 20th Earl of Suffolk in the B.B.C. serial *The Dragon's Opponent*. One of her most recent T.V. appearances was as the runaway wife in Terence Rattigan's *The Deep Blue Sea*.

Married to actor producer Bill Travers, Virginia has four children—and coincidentally played a mother of four in the film version of Arthur Ransome's children's books, *Swallows and Amazons*.

After production work on *Carve her Name with Pride* had been completed, I returned to my role as George Dixon. The growing popularity of the series did not go unnoticed by the police themselves, who liked what they saw of the television bobbies at work and were prepared to co-operate whenever possible. An advertisement in a police publication for ideas for plots brought in no less than twelve hundred stories.

In the early days Dixon's family life, involving his daughter and son-in-law, was no less important to the series than crime investigation, and there was great excitementin 1960 when viewers were introduced to the 'twins' born to Mary and Andy. Jeanette Hutchinson and Peter Byrne received thousands of letters, telegrams and gifts for the 'babies'. Mary's 'pregnancy' was well timed because Jeanette herself was expecting a baby. In fact, her daughter was born only a few weeks after the appearance of the 'twins'.

Further proof of the extraordinary way in which audiences identified with Dixon characters was provided in one episode in the late fifties when Police Constable Bob Penney, played by Tony Parker, now an I.T.V. programme director, was knocked down by a car and later died. Many viewers pleaded for Penney to be brought back to life, as it were, in the next series, but Ted Willis was adamant that he should stay dead. He felt that if *Dixon* was to remain authentic, its stories must truly reflect the work of the police both behind the desk and on the streets where they were exposed to danger. The untimely death of an officer could not be revoked without damaging the credibility of the series.

Among the many calls which jammed the switchboard after this episode was one from a father who said that his seven-year-old son had been so upset by the accident that he couldn't sleep. The child could not be convinced that the policeman was only acting and was certain he had really been killed. Eventually, to reassure and console him, Tony Parker telephoned the youngster and convinced him that his hero was still alive.

In 1958 Dixon, in one of the episodes, was awarded the B.E.M., and I was very touched when a widow in Bristol sent me the medal ribbon of a similar decoration which had belonged to her husband. He was a policeman who had been awarded the medal for bravery in the blitz and she told me in her letter that I was very like him, adding, 'To me, Dixon is real.'

No television programme is ever without its critics, and apparently we upset a teetotal parson who complained to the B.B.C. that Dixon spent all his off-duty hours knocking back beer in the local. He thought that, like the wine-bibbing Rupert Davies in the *Maigret* series, Dixon was setting a bad example and suggested that Maigret and Dixon should sign the pledge. It all sounds a bit ridiculous, especially nowadays, but it does indicate how very careful we have to be not to give offence to viewers whoever they are.

At that time I used to talk a lot about road safety, and delivered a little homily on the subject at the end of each episode. I always told the children to look both ways before stepping off the kerb, and I realised just what my responsibility was when I received a letter which read: 'Dear Mr. Dixon, I like you and your friends at Dock Green very much. Next week will you please say what you said last week about road safety because my brother Willie didn't hear it and he takes more notice of you than he does of our Dad.'

I was always careful to practise what I preached. One night we were filming in a deserted Leadenhall Market, when the script called for me to cross the road to investigate two characters in a parked car. There was no traffic about but I remembered that children would be watching this incident when it reached the television screen, so I carefully carried out the correct kerb drill. I was terribly disconcerted to discover that in the editing of the film, a cut made it appear that I had stepped off the kerb without looking right or left. As I anticipated, I had hundreds of letters from parents and children all giving me a stern wigging.

I like to think that in those days we really succeeded in making children kerb conscious and that now they have grown up, and have families of their own, they have remembered to preach the gospel according to Dixon to their children.

In the early part of 1962, for the first and only time, another actor played the part of George Dixon. It was decided that we should do a flashback to Dixon's early days in the force, showing him as a young constable investigating a case of robbery with violence. The part was played by Desmond Davies, who bore a fair resemblance to me when I was in my early twenties. In this episode, Dixon's wife was still alive and was played by Margaret McCourt.

I wonder how many people remember that the original theme song for the *Dixon* series was, 'Maybe it's Because I'm a Londoner'? It wasn't really suitable because although Dixon's manor was supposed to be in the East End of London, he was really representative of the bobby on the beat in any big town or city. I decided to write some lyrics which I thought would be more appropriate and Jeff Darnell, my old cabaret act partner, composed the music. The end product was the theme song still heard, 'An Ordinary Copper'.

In 1962 the B.B.C. decided that *The Huggetts* on radio had reached the end of the road. It was a wrench for Kathleen Harrison and me to play the last episode together because we had so enjoyed working on the series. The producers asked me to provide a new character in a thirteen-part radio series called *The Motor Way*. I was to play the part of a garage owner, and Peter Byrne was enrolled as my nephew. Versatile Deryck Guyler was cast as the works foreman.

The producer was Geoffrey Owen and we ran into some trouble that could not possibly have been foreseen. The role I was given was really based on the years I had spent in the motor industry and on the life and times of any prominent racing driver. Having recorded the shows, Mollie and I took a well-earned holiday and I remember listening to one of the programmes on my car radio. To my utter astonishment, it had been drastically revised. I was far from happy with it and contacted Geoff to find out what had happened.

I was told that we had no option but to make changes because of a complaint from a listener. Some of the early episodes involved a special racing car to which we had given what we believed was a fictional name. Quite incredibly, a racing car of this name actually existed and the owner had threatened to sue the B.B.C. if the script was not entirely revised and the name of the car and details of it we had broadcast eliminated from all future programmes. This knocked a gaping hole in the entire enterprise and the series failed to get off the ground. My only consolation was that the young son of Raymond Baxter, then B.B.C. motoring correspondent and now well known for his T.V. series *Tomorrow's World*, became one of our fans. At least we had made one listener happy!

The autumn of that year was a time of great sadness for me because my eldest brother, Arthur, died following an operation. I had already heard the news on a day in September when I was driving to the television centre for *Dixon* rehearsals feeling terribly depressed. On the way I happened to catch a glimpse of Frankie Howerd whom I had known for many years. As I had not seen him for some time I pulled into the kerb to talk to him.

Frankie is an extremely sensitive and gentle man, and as I wound down the window of my car and hailed him he gave me a warm smile. Suddenly I realised that I could not return his greeting. He could see I was distressed and without a word got into the car and I told him what had happened. His fans, and they are legion, know him only as a marvellously entertaining comedian impossible to plagiarise, but beyond the footlights there are aspects to his character that reveal a warmth and understanding one always hopes to find in a friend. His advice and sympathy on that afternoon helped to alleviate the misery I felt and enabled me again to face up to my work programme that day. Frankie himself has known the grief of personal loss in the death of his mother to whom he was devoted. It was some time before he was able to renew his life.

I first met Frankie at the time he made his initial appearance in radio's *Variety Bandbox* in 1947 when I happened to be the only person sitting in the stalls as he rehearsed for the show at Camberwell Palace. I thought he was very, very funny, and I would have roared my head off had I not felt self-conscious among all those vacant seats.

The boys in the orchestra had been playing for a long time and didn't take much notice of him. I wasn't really surprised at their lack of response because as I knew from years of experience, musicians are always intent upon their own job. Their chief worry is timing. If they are fractionally out with their entry—such as coming in with a drum roll, a ripped-off blast from the trombones or trumpets or a full orchestral chord—they can ruin a comedian's timing of a joke. I sensed that Frankie was not too happy so I went round to his dressing room and sure enough, I found him in a very gloomy mood. Like Tony Hancock and Reg Varney in their time, Frankie was convinced that he hadn't what it takes. I did what I could to allay his fear and told him that his act was in a class of its own and could not help but succeed.

What happened to him is only too well known. He became resident star of *Variety Bandbox* and succeeded brilliantly until 1958 when, as occurs to most of us at one time or another, he hit a very bad patch indeed. For three years he was more often out of work than in, but it took only a single appearance in the late-night satirical show, *That Was the Week That Was*, to restore him to public esteem.

There is nothing quite as individual as comedy, but although no comedian can hope to please all the people all the time there are a few who come very close to achieving this ideal. In this category I would place Frankie Howerd, Dick Emery and Jimmy Edwards as well as Tony Hancock, Sid Field, and one of my personal favourites, Jimmy Wheeler, who died after a heart attack in October, 1973.

I knew Jimmy and his father, Ernie Wilson, very well. For a long time they were teamed as a double act, Wheeler and

Wilson, and were featured in one of the first *Garrison Theatre* shows. Ernie dressed up as a sailor and Jimmy played the part of a railway porter; both possessed a spontaneous sense of humour which effervesced off stage as well as on.

Jimmy started in the business by winning a clog-dancing competition at the age of five. Charlie Chaplin, then unknown, wanted to take him to America with him but instead, Jimmy and his father worked together until Ernie Wilson died just after the last war. Jimmy went solo and soon became famous for his catch phrase, 'Aye, aye, that's your lot!' It was heard during thirty appearances at the London Palladium and at five Royal Variety shows. One of his last appearances was with my sisters, Elsie and Doris, in a season of music-hall at Greenwich.

It was in 1962—a mixed year for me—that I made my last film. I had greatly enjoyed my years in the movies and it was with some regret that I decided my television commitments precluded serious involvement elsewhere.

I was still in the force, so to speak, in my final film as a detective-inspector investigating a murder in Brighton. The thriller was called *Jigsaw* and I found it amusing to watch when it appeared recently as a late-night movie on B.B.C.

It was shot on location in and around Brighton with the full co-operation of the Sussex police. Val Guest not only wrote the screenplay but directed and produced the picture. The cast included Yolande Donlan, Moira Redmond, Ronald Lewis and John le Mesurier.

The year 1962 was also the diamond jubilee of the Sutton Amateur Dramatic Club at which I had been given my first opportunity to appear on stage as a straight actor. To mark the occasion I had organised a variety show the receipts from which were donated to club funds. Among the stars who appeared on that memorable evening were Frankie Howerd, Cyril Fletcher and Anne Shelton. As compere I was more than a little husky having, quite suddenly, developed an attack of laryngitis. I had to ditch my solo spot.

CHAPTER 13

Dixon of Dock Green

IT WOULDN'T surprise me if someone suggested that George Dixon was my *alter ego* because I have always believed there existed an affinity between us. Micky Balcon seemed to think so when he cast me for the role in *The Blue Lamp*. Conversely, you could say that the Dixon in the television series is uncannily like Jack Warner. The thought occurred to me for the first time in 1963 when the future of the eight-year-old series suddenly became uncertain. Ted Willis, who had written over two hundred episodes, announced that the current series would be his last, and explained that he felt he was becoming stale and wanted to try something new. He was already involved in writing a number of plays for television and had provided the script for a picture to be made by a film company he had just founded in Australia. In addition, he was producing two new series, the *Sergeant Cork* stories and *Taxi*, starring Sid James.

When Ted's intentions became known, Tom Sloan, head of B.B.C. light entertainment, was in America, and we had to wait an agonising three weeks for his return before the fate of

Dixon was determined. Needless to say, I was delighted by the decision to continue the series with a new team of script-writers, because Dixon had become part of my life. He was real to me and also to many viewers who took the trouble to write to 'Dixon'. Ever since they got to know him viewers have shown a great affection for this ordinary copper—an affection, I am happy to say, which has rubbed off on Jack Warner.

It was confirmed beyond doubt when I was taken ill during the filming of an episode in the days when the series went out live. I had been feeling pretty rough all day and as the screening was almost at an end the place started to spin round and to my horror I just couldn't remember my lines. I am told that I swayed and put a hand to my head. The cameras quickly switched to Peter Byrne, who covered up in a highly professional manner by delivering some of my lines. I was taken home and confined to bed for some days suffering from a bout of influenza at its worst. I was told that I could not have arrived at our mews flat before the B.B.C. switchboard was jammed with callers anxious to know what was wrong with me. One man who telephoned later explained that he had had to walk four miles to his nearest call box. Within the next two days Mollie and I received over 3,000 letters from viewers wishing me a speedy recovery.

I like to think that our series has done something towards making people aware of the tricks criminals get up to. An elderly lady living in West London was conned into letting three strange men 'tidy up' her garden and was horrified when they demanded something like £100 for the job. She was too frightened to refuse to pay and wrote out a cheque for the amount. One of the tricksters then deliberately smudged her signature and ordered her to write another cheque on the pretence that the bank would not accept an unclear signature. They also forced her to issue a letter of authority enabling them to collect the money in cash.

The villains successfully presented one of the cheques for payment but were unlucky when they tried to collect on the second. They presented it to a bank clerk who was a Dixon fan and had seen this particular trick exposed on the programme. He checked the clients' account, confirmed a previous payment for a like amount, and then alerted the police. At least there were three fewer con men at large for a time!

Another episode in the serial provided a warning to elderly people that thieves were posing as meter readers or representatives of the local authority to gain entry. The routine trick was for one of them to keep the householder chatting while the other dodged from one room to another picking up what he could. The police were very appreciative of the programme and, on their suggestion, it was repeated.

Unfortunately, a lot of trusting souls are so gullible that they become easy prey, but I think the episode caused many to exercise more care and to demand evidence of identification from mystery callers. Quite a number of viewers wrote to me saying they had bought front-door chains as a protection against doubtful visitors.

Similarly, in the early days of the series, a number of programmes were directed towards young people with the do-s and don't-s unobtrusively presented. On a train journey I once made from Lowestoft to Liverpool Street I saw some children darting out of their back gardens on to the railway lines. I was so horrified at the possible consequences of their dangerous game that, in collaboration with my producer, a warning against the practice was worked into one of the programmes. I had many letters from parents thanking me for putting across a message that might easily save the lives of many children.

For several years I presented safe cycling awards to pupils at St. Paul's Junior School, London, and I always told them that when they graduated to driving motor cars the same safety rules would apply. I advised them to be careful because any fool could drive fast, but there was a time and a place for this kind of expertise.

It is quite common for people to write to me about their problems with wayward children. When first I received such confidences I was a little surprised and perplexed. After all, I could scarcely claim to be a probation officer or a child psychologist and I wasn't quite sure how to handle the situation. Eventually I decided that if the children really did believe in George Dixon, there was no reason why I should not write to them and offer the kind of advice an old village bobby might have given verbally, accompanied by a few wags of a beefy finger. Letters I received later from harassed parents indicated that my brief homilies had had the desired effect. The Mother Superior of a convent school for delinquents once told me that a few words from Dixon at the conclusion of a programme had more impact on them than much of the advice they received from the sisters.

We have, of course, had our share of embarrassing moments in the filming of various episodes. On one occasion we had a sound technician in the boot of a car, and when a re-take became necessary the poor chap had become extremely uncomfortable. He wasn't getting enough air and solved his dilemma by opening the boot lid a fraction and dangling one foot outside

An alert and public-spirited passer-by noticed the foot and telephoned the police, greatly agitated, to advise them that he had seen a car go by carrying a body in the boot. . . .

There were red faces all round but the real cops were very understanding.

There was another incident when a street trader raised his arms threateningly to a child who was supposed to have annoyed him. A man walking by took exception to this and was all set for a punch-up when the barrow-boy managed to gasp, 'Hold it! Hold it! I'm an actor and so is the boy.'

In another episode which demanded my presence on point duty in Notting Hill, I began by watching a real police constable directing traffic. At that precise moment, however, a young girl breathlessly rushed towards me and complained that a man was following her. I turned around and saw that he was still coming, and he was indeed a very large and unpleasant looking character. I don't quite know what would have transpired had not the real policeman realised my dilemma. He nipped smartly across to me and told me to get into the road and hold up the traffic. The girl then crossed the street while the officer held back the other pedestrians, including her pursuer. By the time he had signalled me to let the traffic flow again the girl had vanished and so, too, had her pursuer. It was a nice example of spontaneous co-operation between Dixon and the genuine policeman. I was even more amused when I returned to the pavement and was approached by a smiling lady who remarked, 'My, aren't you like Dixon of Dock Green? You should be on television!'

I suffered a further embarrassment about this time, but as Jack Warner and not Dixon.

I was flabbergasted to learn in 1963, via the columns of a Scottish newspaper, that Dixon of Dock Green had won £50,000 during an eight-day gambling spree in Le Touquet! I was supposed to have been the member of a baccarat syndicate including film producer Darryl Zanuck and two other men.

In a letter to the paper I wrote, 'I was delighted to read that Jack Warner had won £50,000 . . . unfortunately, however, the Jack Warner you mentioned was not Dixon of Dock Green but Jack L. Warner the film magnate. I am not a millionaire —how can I be on a copper's pay?'

The newspaper published a correction and apology and no great harm was done. Despite what is alleged about the Scots being opportunists I didn't receive a single begging letter from readers who had been told of my big win!

Some fairly significant changes took place in *Dixon* during the next couple of years. Jeanette Hutchinson, who had been with us as Mary, left the series to go to Australia with her husband and little girl in the spring of 1964. She was written out by being sent to Canada for a holiday. When we returned to the screen in the autumn I had a new daughter, Anna Dawson, and of course, Peter Byrne had a new wife. She stayed with us for just one series. It was her first big acting role on the small screen.

Gradually it became more difficult than ever to find stories into which the family could be naturally introduced and by the following year they had practically disappeared. Jeanette returned from Australia—with two additional children—and she took over her old part for just three episodes. But ultimately, 'Andy' and 'Mary' moved with the twins to Chelmsford, from which Andy supposedly commuted daily to Dock Green. So far as the viewer was concerned, apart from brief domestic references, the family never figure in the programmes.

As I mentioned earlier, I'm a little sorry we had to drop the family situations but if they re-appeared now, the twins would be fourteen!

I had no idea the series would enjoy such a long T.V. life and it was certainly never intended that P.C. Dixon would ever receive promotion. Nevertheless its viewing figures were better than ever, and it would have been illogical to suppose I had not qualified for promotion after my long stint. My rise in rank was linked with the changing face of the series. Recently Peter Byrne made me realise how greatly all of us had changed. He had just seen a re-run of one of the early episodes and was amused by it. He said, 'At the end of the story you walked down the steps of the station, looked at the stars and remarked that that was the end of the tale—'They locked him up and I'm now going to have a beer. . . .'

'It wasn't a bit like Dixon,' Peter told me, 'you were more like a comic or a clown. And did you realise that in those days we all spoke with pronounced Cockney accents?'

I hadn't realised we had ever used any particular accent. I haven't got a Cockney accent or for that matter what used to be called an Oxford or B.B.C. one. Mine is just straightforward London. Very few people have tried to impersonate me and among those who did I would say that Florence Desmond, one of the lovely great impressionists, and Ernest Shannon—he was a regular listener to *Garrison Theatre*—were the most successful.

Ernest died in 1966 and to my amazement he bequeathed to me his considerable collection of records although I had not seen him for around twenty years.

The year 1965 was one which I look back upon with some pride because it was then that I was made an O.B.E. in the Queen's Birthday Honours List. Several other members of my profession received recognition that year, including veteran actor Felix Aylmer, who received a knighthood. Two other recipients of the O.B.E. were Frankie Vaughan and Violet Carson of *Coronation Street.* She was equally well known years ago when she played the piano for Wilfred Pickles in radio's *Have a Go* programmes.

The investiture in the State Ballroom at Buckingham Palace was a memorable occasion. I suppose most people imagine it would be difficult not to be overawed in such circumstances. I found the whole atmosphere dignified but very warm and friendly. The formality of the red carpet was completely diminished by the pleasant background music played as we were presented to Her Majesty. When she greeted me, she said, 'I always watch your programme and I've often wondered if you get very tired appearing in a show each week?' I assured her quite truthfully that I enjoyed the work and that the change in the story line each week added variety to the role I played.

In the somewhat toughened version of *Dixon* in the sixties, I received a gunshot wound towards the end of the first episode of a two-part story and that really put the cat among the pigeons. Viewers were to be kept in suspense until the following week when they would learn whether or not my injury had proved fatal, but there were so many telephone calls to the B.B.C. that within twenty-four hours it was decided that an official 'bulletin' would have to be issued.

Viewers telephoning were told, 'When the story is continued next week, Sergeant Dixon will still be critically ill. His life will hang in the balance, but he will not die.'

One of the things I found most touching about this affair was the number of 'Don't let Dixon die' letters sent in by children and read in *Junior Points of View*. I also received many personal telephone calls and letters, including this one from a little girl: 'Dear Mr. Dixon, I love you and your friends at Dock Green very much. I always go to the toilet when they hurt you and come out when the nasty part is over. . . .'

The smoke from the gun play had barely vanished when yet another gratifying tribute was paid to the homely bobby. The Variety Club of Great Britain announced that I was to receive a special award for starring in the longest-running T.V. crime series—in itself adjudged to be a programme calculated to produce the most social benefits.

There were inevitably a few snide remarks when I received my next award—5,000 members of Mrs. Mary Whitehouse's National Viewers' and Listeners' Association voted Dixon the most suitable programme for family viewing. I accepted the award, a silver sculpture, on behalf of the *Dixon* team. Quite a number of people asked me if I was not embarrassed by the acknowledgement from people regarded by some as a bunch of straight-laced do-gooders, but I could see no reason to be ashamed of taking part in a clean show from which sex and violence were absent. I have considerable sympathy with Mrs. Whitehouse and her aims. Anyone trying to clean up entertainment and bring about the elimination of distasteful scenes has my support. Millions of people have to be satisfied in this respect and if the networks aren't careful they will offend more than they delight.

I understand that one of the reasons the *Dixon* series has never been sold to American T.V. networks is because it is regarded as too soft. The Americans—at least those who have never toured this country—cannot believe that our policemen don't carry arms except in very special circumstances. I think that the programme would be successful in the U.S.A. if given a trial run because I have a lot of friends there who are convinced it would provide a pleasant change from what is now being shown. One person who holds this view is Raymond Burr, the famous star of *A Man Called Ironside*.

I met Raymond in 1970 when he flew here to say thank you to the millions of British fans who have ensured his programme a place in the top T.V. ratings. With Peter Byrne and Stratford Johns and Frank Windsor, of the *Softly Softly* team, I had a long chat with Raymond at the T.V. Centre. He told me he had been making public appearances in twenty-six countries in connection with his series and couldn't understand why *Dixon* was not sold abroad, particularly because of the international success of *The Blue Lamp*.

Raymond is a most charming man who now spends much of his leisure time on a little island he has bought near Fiji in the South Seas, where he rears cattle, ducks and pigs, and concerns himself with the islanders' welfare. Mollie and I have a standing invitation to visit him there and maybe one day I'll be able to take it up.

He is a man for whom I have a lot of admiration because he has reached the top of his profession despite the tragic events in his private life. Canadian by birth, Raymond toured Britain with a repertory company when he was a young actor and met and married an English girl, Annette Sutherland. He suffered a terrible blow by her death during the war. She was a passenger on the same aeroplane with actor Leslie Howard which was shot down by German fighters over the Bay of Biscay while on a flight to London. Raymond and Annette had one child, a boy, who lived in Britain with his grandparents after the death of his mother. He died of leukemia at the age of ten. Ray's second marriage ended in divorce and his third wife died of cancer. He is passionately fond of children and has accepted responsibility for seventeen war orphans under the Foster Parents' Plan and similar organisations.

His enormous following here was established in the *Perry Mason* series in which he became television's most famous lawyer. Less than two years after they ceased he was back on the screen as Ironside. Before his portrayal as the paraplegic crime-fighter he visited many veteran and military hospitals in America to gain first-hand knowledge of the problems which beset those confined to wheelchairs. In fact, he has had personal experience of disability. He was partially paralysed for a year after being wounded in the last war and he told me it helped him to get into the skin of Ironside.

I was reminded once again of the failure to exploit Dixon abroad when Mollie and I visited Rhodesia in the spring of 1971. Viewers there were able to see *Softly Softly*, *Z Cars*, *All Gas and Gaiters* and *Dr. Finlay's Casebook*—but not *Dixon of Dock Green.* This appeared very strange to me because so many people there had left England only ten or eleven years earlier and had been *Dixon* fans.

We went to Rhodesia to visit some friends who at one time had little reason to welcome our presence. Before the second war we lived at one time in a first-floor flat in Greencroft Gardens, Hampstead, and above the one occupied by a Mr. and Mrs. Jack Day. In those days I would spend hours bashing away at an old typewriter on which I produced my scripts—and it was far from being a silent model! I don't know how long the Days suffered before they finally pointed out that the noise and vibration of the typewriter was disrupting their otherwise peaceful lives. I was terribly sorry when I realised what a nuisance I had been and solved the problem by buying a thick rubber mat to put beneath the machine. Happily, there was no more disturbance and Mollie and I became firm friends with the Days. In fact, when their son was born, they asked me to be his godfather and he was christened John Warner Day.

The family emigrated to Rhodesia twenty-five years ago but our friendship has never waned. They have constantly invited us over but it was 1971 before we finally made it. There occurred a very happy reunion at their home in Salisbury and I was delighted to hear that my godson held the distinction of being the youngest captain in Air Rhodesia. What started as a holiday developed into a working trip as well, because once people learned I was there, I received requests to do radio and television shows.

In our tour we included a visit to Victoria Falls and a call on

Mr. Ian Smith whose parting words to me were, 'Will you tell your friends in London that we are still very proud of our heritage?'

One of my last social engagements before making the Rhodesian trip gave me the opportunity to meet once again the man who indirectly had played quite an important part in my life, the great Maurice Chevalier, then aged eighty-two. The occasion was Foyles' Literary Luncheon at the Dorchester to launch Maurice's memoirs, appropriately titled, *I Remember it Well*, and it really was a gala event. I was at the top table with Ingrid Bergman, the equally lovely and gracious Dame Anna Neagle, Herbert Wilcox, Vera Lynn, Bob Monkhouse, Dora Bryan, Diana Napier (Richard Tauber's widow), Patricia Burke and impresarios Bernard Delfont and Emile Littler.

Anna Neagle proposed a toast to 'one of the real immortals, a very great entertainer', and I couldn't help feeling a little nostalgic for my youthful days in Paris when I spent my last franc on that visit to see the 'new entertainer', Maurice Chevalier.

Later that year, in December, 1971, I had the honour to be invited to Buckingham Palace again, this time to take part in a Christmas entertainment arranged by Anona Winn for the 'Not Forgotten Association', a branch of the British Legion which provides funds for wounded soldiers of the two world wars. The show was held in the riding school at the Palace before the Duchess of Kent, and among my fellow artistes were Evelyn Laye, Nicholas Parsons and Dora Bryan. I like to keep busy and these social and charity events are just little extras that come along and keep me in trim as a solo entertainer.

My Dixon activities don't allow me to take part in any other regular show and I suppose I've been pushed into something of a corner but it's a place I like. I have turned down many offers to appear in West End plays over the years and I would still like to do one, but while the B.B.C. continue to need me for Dixon I'm happy to stay. I've no regrets. The series has provided me with a steady income all these years, for which

I'm grateful, but it's become more than a meal ticket. It's part of my life—and not a small part!

Inevitably, there have been suggestions that I should retire from the force simply because I'm now too old to be a copper. Why can't people be satisfied that I'm fit and well and let me get on with my job? If the critics care to think about the situation, they would realise that when I made the first *Dixon* series in 1955, I was already approaching the retirement age of the ordinary Metropolitan Police bobby. I see no reason why I should not carry on as George Dixon while the B.B.C. has fifteen million viewers happy to watch the programme.

There was once an idea that if the *Dixon* series came off—this was when it had run six years—I should play the part of a security officer in a big store in a new series. I didn't care for the project and I didn't hesitate to say so. If there ever is a plan to follow-up *Dixon* I should like the role of a retired copper who has bought a little shop in the country. I could have a housekeeper—who knows, it might even be Kathleen Harrison?—take walks and ride a bike and call upon anyone plagued by a spot of trouble—the sort of thing an old ex-policeman would do. It would probably be a bit of a blend between *Dixon* and *The Archers*. I think such a series has its possibilities.

In the meantime, the series continues to pull in awards. In 1971, the Joint Industries Committee of Television Advertising Research listed *Dixon* as the most popular B.B.C. show. The following year the Top Ten T.V. Ratings for the London area named the programme as number one, beating *Colditz* and *Dad's Army*, which tied for second place.

January, 1973, brought me a special award as Britain's best-loved cop from the Variety Club of Great Britain. I received it at the club's annual awards dinner held at 'The Talk of the Town'. On the same night, Dick Emery was voted B.B.C. T.V. Personality of the Year. Unhappily, he was taken ill a day or two before the event and watched the presentation on television from his hospital bed.

My latest 'award' was something quite different but one of which I am extremely proud. In February, 1973, I was made a Freeman of the City of London, an honour which entitles me to a set of eighteenth-century Rules For the Conduct of Life urging me to be sober and temperate. Not too difficult with Dixon to keep an eye on me!

CHAPTER 14

My very Good Friends

I'VE BEEN lucky in so many ways.

Lucky to have been born of wonderful parents into a happy family circle, lucky to have been encouraged to develop the talent I possessed, which enabled me to earn my living in a way which has happily combined profit with pleasure. Often I was lucky to be in the right place at the right time, and also in the chances that came to provide the kind of entertainment the public wanted, at the appropriate time.

But most of all I have been lucky with the people in my life. People like Maurice Sizaire, my mentor, from whom I learned much more than a knowledge of thoroughbred motor-cars; Nelson Darling, alias Jeff Darnell, with whom I first appeared on stage in the Collaborators' Concert Party at 'ye old village fayre' at Cheam Park in Surrey, in 1927; Bobby Alderson, my pianist and friend for so many years; my agent and 'nurse-maid', John McMichael; and way above all others, my wife Mollie.

Jeff Darnell is a man of many parts. As well as being a schoolmaster and the instrumental half of Warner and Darnell for many years, he has been an amateur sportsman, singer, businessman and soldier with a distinguished record in two world wars. As a boy he was a chorister at Peterborough Cathedral and was soprano soloist at many concerts. At King's School, Peterborough, he was King's Scholar in 1910 with distinctions in Latin, modern languages and English, as well as being prominent in many sports. Jeff had always intended to become a schoolmaster, but his studies were interrupted by World War I in which he enlisted in the Northamptonshire Regiment and was commissioned early in 1915. He was awarded the Military Cross and was three times mentioned in despatches before being demobilised with the rank of Staff Captain.

On his return to civilian life Jeff began teaching at Sutton, but retained his sporting interests, playing cricket for Sutton and touring with Northants Amateurs. He also ran his own dance band from 1921 to 1937. In 1922 he was invited by Eric Ansell, son of Composer John Ansell, to join the Collaborators' Concert Party which put on shows for charity. I was introduced to Jeff, and this led to a partnership which continued on the amateur and professional stage until 1938, when I decided to go it alone in show business. Jeff pursued his career as a teacher by day and entertainer by night until September, 1939. He was on the reserve of officers and was sent to France early in October as Staff Officer H.Q. 1st Corps. Jeff was Town Major at Arras G.H.Q. when the first German bomb dropped on the town landed just outside his billet and blew him out of bed. He had a pretty hectic time during the German advance and in May, 1940, was on board the last destroyer to leave Dunkirk.

Back in England Jeff was promoted to the rank of First Grade Staff Officer War Office, and as personal representative of the Adjutant General, Sir Ronald Adam. In 1945 he was appointed Assistant Adjutant General Southern Command under General Sir John Crooker and later General (now Field-Marshal) Sir John Harding and two years later was demobilised with the rank of Lieutenant-Colonel.

Jeff did not return to teaching but went into business.

Although he retired in 1967 he still has a part-time job as secretary of a working men's club.

Bobby Alderson made his stage debut almost by accident. As a young private in the Royal Sussex Regiment in occupation on the Rhine just after World War I he volunteered to help out when a concert party needed a pianist. He says he only did so to avoid drills and humdrum duties! Anyway, by the time he was demobilised he had acquired a taste for show business and in 1921 joined Jack Hylton's first orchestra. He left after three years because he felt his true role was that of an accompanist. His talents were quickly recognised and he was the man at the piano for Clarice Mayne for six years and also for Phyllis Dare, Carl Brisson, Stanley Holloway, Elsie Carlisle and Florence Desmond.

Bobby spent two years with Stanley Holloway in the original *Co-Optimists*, one of the famous concert parties of the years between the wars, and in 1937 he joined the Fol-de-Rols. We teamed up together in 1938 and he has been with me ever since, at the piano whenever I need an accompanist and often as secretary.

I am not the only member of the Waters family to be grateful for Bobby's skill on the keyboard. During the 1939–45 war he toured all over the world with Elsie and Doris, entertaining servicemen. Of course he was with me in Korea and Japan in 1951 and in the same year went to the Middle East with Leslie Henson.

Many people have been kind enough to describe me as an amiable person but I know that I can become intolerant—whenever I encounter phoneys. I can't stand people who put on airs and graces or members of the profession who achieve success and become conceited and boorish. Some of the nicest people I have met in my life have had scarcely two pennies to rub together but I have warmed to them because of their sincerity and honesty.

I wouldn't suggest that John McMichael, who became my agent in 1957, is by any means a pauper and he wouldn't want me to pretend that he hasn't employed some bluff during his career. But John is a character with a great sense of humour and a man who is completely honest about his life. He was one of those unfortunate young men who was caught up in the last war and courageously gave of his best before he had a chance to carve out a future for himself

When war was declared in 1939 John was on holiday in his last year at school. He says that 'in an attempt to opt out of responsibility, like a lot of other young fellows', he volunteered for service with the army at seventeen. He wasn't called up until December, 1940, when he joined the 10th Hussars where 'by good behaviour and good luck I managed to ease myself into Sandhurst'. He was commissioned in January, 1941, after only three months' training as an officer cadet.

Scientists had discovered that if a sufficiently tall piece of canvas was wrapped around a tank it would float and also that by connecting the propeller to the gearbox, the tank became a motorised 'craft'. The regiment John was with spent three years developing the water-born tanks that were to be used three years later in the assault on the Normandy beaches on June 6th, 1944.

I recall John giving me an account of the landing. He said: 'It was all very effective. The Jerries assumed that what they were seeing were small canvas boats heading for the beaches and only realised they were tanks when the canvas screens were dropped. Unfortunately, nobody volunteered the vital information that morning that we were heading for the beach as the tide was coming in. As I was more interested in what was happening in front of me rather than behind, when I dropped my screen we were flooded. But at least we didn't sink. . . .'

John was in action until V.E. Day and was twice mentioned in despatches although he dismisses this as airily as he does the fact that he survived in a regiment with an enormous casualty rate. When he left the service at the age of twenty-four, he had attained the rank of major and was earning £1,200 a year.

'After I had been demobilised, it seemed that I was destined to live on my wits, so far as a career was concerned,' he explained. Unable to speak a word of German, he obtained a post with the Rank organisation—as a German translator! Somehow he managed to get by until he gently eased himself into what was called the Special Services Department where he became involved with the personal appearances of some of the one hundred and sixteen contract players with the Rank Organisation.

He quickly learned the value of just talking and once told Stewart Granger that he knew Winston Churchill very well. Although he had never met Britain's war leader he managed to effect an introduction and acquired a reputation as the man who knew everybody. It was during 1947 that he met me for the first time.

A few years later John became very depressed and dissatisfied with his somewhat odd position in the Rank Organisation, and I asked him if he would like to go with me on the Korean trip. He jumped at the chance.

Shortly after the tour, John went to Rome, where he became a theatrical agent, later returning to this country to join Associated Rediffusion for a couple of years before taking a job with Connie's Ltd., the theatrical and film agency. For ten years he represented me and finally, in 1968, established his own business, handling my affairs as well as those of Richard Harris and Stanley Baker.

Of course the luckiest break of my life was my meeting with the girl who was to become my wife, Mollie Peters. She says the first thing she noticed about me was the shiny seat of my trousers, but it evidently didn't put her off! What first impressed me about her was her lovely speaking voice, so gentle and calm. We were engaged for about four years before our marriage at St. Mark's Church, Regent's Park, on November 23rd, 1933. We didn't need even a single carriage for the event because the church was just across the road from my home. We had only a three-day honeymoon before both returning to work.

Mollie's father was a Scot from Aberdeen who came to London when he was nineteen and married a London girl. Mollie was the youngest of their ten children. Towards the end of the first war she trained as a shorthand typist and got a job at the Ministry of Munitions, before moving on to other secretarial posts including that at Lendrum and Hartman in Albemarle Street, where I first saw her. Her secretarial experience has been invaluable to me because she manages the business side of my affairs, looking after income tax, royalties and personal appearances. People are always telephoning me at home when I am at the studio and Mollie doesn't just make a list of messages. She sorts things out, keeps me up to date wherever I am and rings me if there is something urgent that I should know.

She can read me like a book now and never, so to speak, puts a foot wrong. I often keep a script by the bed in order to make changes in the dialogue that I feel necessary. Usually I sleep very well, but I can't do so if some little thing in the script is niggling me.

Lots of women would get narked at having their sleep disturbed, but Mollie knows that if I switch on the bedside light I am doing it for a good reason. She makes everything terribly easy for me. If I had someone on my back telling me what I should do or not do it would make my job very difficult, but Mollie just goes jogging along in her quiet way. Whenever I go up in the air for no real reason—though not as often as I used to—Mollie has a calming influence. Bad manners make me furious, but Mollie whispers, 'Take no notice' and I know she is right.

She has never questioned what I have done or planned, or been jealous of the attention I get from all kinds of people. She accompanies me to concerts and other functions and enjoys them as much as I do. The more I think about it the more fantastic it seems—that I should have someone beside me who always does the right thing. Mollie only worries if she thinks I am taking on too many engagements. Sometimes I'm asked to appear at as many as sixteen charity functions in a single day, mostly on Saturdays in the summer. Obviously it is impossible to be present at all of them but I do my best.

Some wives would have beefed about their husbands going to Korea in the middle of a war, but Mollie accepted the situation and its dangers when I told her I was going out there to entertain the troops. She just asked, 'What will you be taking with you?'

She backs me up, too, if I want to do something that might be financially risky. For instance, she encouraged me to go ahead when I was offered the part of Dixon in *The Blue Lamp*, although so many of my friends thought I was foolish to accept such a small part. It's not a question of saying what she hopes will please me; if she doesn't agree with me she says so and more often than not she's dead right.

Mollie is a big help when I'm reading scripts. In a job like mine it's nothing but words and more words, and often it is difficult to see through the verbal maze. She can view problems much more objectively and often suggests script changes that make all the difference.

I could not have wished for a better wife or working partner. When we were first married we had a little flat near my garage. It was a tricky time financially and Mollie kept her job in the city to help pay the bills. I caught a bad chill driving an open car up to Scotland and simply had to take to my bed. Every day Mollie came home to give me my lunch before hurrying back to work. I didn't want her to do it but she insisted. On another occasion when I took Mollie to see her sister I felt so rotten that I had to go to bed at her sister's house. I had driven there in a big American car I had been testing for my employers and I suppose Mollie knew I would be a bit worried about returning it. When I awoke at one o'clock in the morning she was standing beside the bed. She had only had a few driving lessons, but she had driven the car back to the West End, garaged it where it belonged, then returned to her sister's house by train and bus just to find out how I was. It was a nightmare trip for her because she was very inexperienced and the roads were icy after a lot of snow.

She is a very undemanding person in every way and has never been greedy for the material things of life. The wives of many men in my position would want a new dress for every function—but not her. I don't have to cough up three or four hundred quid every time we go out, because Mollie is quite happy to remodel something out of her wardrobe. She's not mean but she takes a pride in being thrifty. Often she gives me a bit of a wink when someone congratulates her on a lovely new gown!

When things began to improve after the lean times, I was happy to know that I could now give Mollie a few of life's goodies. I promised her a fur coat when I started at the Palladium, but she preferred to wait until she thought I could really afford it, and even then she chose an inexpensive one. It was a long time before I bought her a mink.

In one series of *Dixon* we did a lot of filming in very cold conditions and most of the cast were wearing ski suits or long pants. One afternoon I said to Mollie, 'We're out filming again tonight and it's going to be damn cold. I wish I still had those long pants I wore in Norway.' She didn't say a word, but from goodness knows where she unearthed those I had worn when filming *Valley of the Eagles* about fifteen years before. Molly is certainly a bit of a hoarder.

Mollie has many talents and lots of interests. She sings very well and I am sure could have made a name for herself on the stage or concert platform. When she left school she won a singing scholarship which, had she been able to take it up, would have paid half the fees for professional training. However, she went into business instead but found an outlet for her talents by joining an amateur dramatic society and singing in musical comedy. Later she decided to take lessons and went to one of the best teachers in London, Miss Lucille Benstead, a famous music-hall star with a wonderful voice. Miss Benstead had been a child prodigy and when she was only five years old was sent from her home in Alice Springs, Australia to be trained in Paris. She sang all over the world and even today is a marvellous teacher and a great character at eighty-three. The well-known song 'Chloe' was specially written for Lucille, the 'The Bells of St. Mary's' was composed in her drawing room and she was the singer who introduced the evergreen 'There's a Long Long Trail a Winding'. Mollie has sung with me at charity concerts—and people often say how wonderful it is that she still has the voice of a young woman.

Another of her talents is sketching in pen and ink, but most of her activities nowadays centre on our home in Kent. Sometimes I return there after being away and find she's practically pulled the place down, making all sorts of improvements she's had in mind for a long time.

Luck again—or fate if you like—played a part in our acquisition of our home. Many years ago, when the Waters family would take an annual holiday at Herne Bay, I often thought that I'd like to live in that part of Kent if ever I had the chance. In 1946 Mollie and I took a short break and stayed at the Kingsgate Castle Hotel, near Broadstairs. While we were there I visited the local golf course and had a chat with the secretary, Colonel Broadwood. I asked him to tip me off if he heard of any cottages that were coming on to the market and it wasn't long before he wrote to say there was a small lodge for sale near the golf course at Kingsgate. We looked at it and thought it very nice but was really too small for our needs. As we were talking to the agent I glanced across the garden and saw an old wreck of a place—the ramshackle stables to the original mansion. I jokingly asked if they were for sale and to my surprise the agent said they were. Immediately he showed me some drawings and the already approved conversion plans and said, 'That's what it will look like when it's finished.' We inspected the ruin and practically bought it on the spot. Mollie persuaded the builders to make a few changes and so we got just what we wanted. I was also able to acquire some extra land so that we have a three-bedroomed cottage with lounge, dining room, kitchen, bathroom and garage, standing in one and a half acres. There is a lawn, part of which is used for croquet, a small orchard, kitchen garden and copse at the side. Beyond an ancient flint wall with a lychgate is the North Foreland Golf Course. We had quite a problem naming the cottage. Nothing suitable came to mind until I had a sudden inspiration. When I was a little lad I used to call horses 'porses'. So Porsea Cottage it became. We have travelled all over the world and seen some fabulous sights, but Mollie and I agree that the most wonderful sight ever is the first glimpse of Porsea Cottage as we arrive home.

We also have a flat in town, because when I am working on *Dixon* there's very little opportunity to visit the cottage. I hate living in hotels and it would be even worse to travel to London from Kingsgate every day.

For a few years we had a third home—a boat moored at Thames Ditton. The idea was that when I was working in London, and unable to get to Kingsgate, we could spend weekends and some free time on the river. I must say it was very peaceful and relaxing, even though I seemed to be reading *Dixon* scripts most of the time, and we had some very nice trips on the Thames. I thought of buying a bigger boat so that we could cross to France and go down the French canals, but in fact we never got further than Windsor. Plans to go right up river to Oxford and explore the waterways there sadly came to nothing. There just wasn't enough time available and for two years we used the boat only twice a year, which was a sheer waste of money. Eventually I sold it.

Mollie has always been very keen on cars, and when I first began to take her out she had a trick of hanging on to the side, as though the car was being driven too fast for her liking. But that wasn't so because she still does the same thing today. I decided at the time that I would teach her to drive. I gave her two or three lessons, then we went to Regent's Park and I got out and I told her, 'You're on your own now.' There wasn't nearly as much traffic on the road in those days, but even so I panicked as soon as she moved off. I tried to call her back but she had gone and it seemed like an eternity until she returned. Never have I been so pleased to see an approaching car than when Mollie got back safe and sound behind the wheel. Since then she's developed into a marvellous driver.

I've never lost my passion for cars and I like reading motor magazines, especially the old ones. I should love to possess an old Sizaire-Berwick, but it would cost a fortune even if I could find one. It was a wonderful car. I'm also still pretty mad about horses and retain a schoolboy's enthusiasm for Western films and books. For equally obvious reasons, I suppose, I like a good detective novel and am a great fan of Agatha Christie.

Mollie and I visit Porsea Cottage as often as we can, where we play a lot of croquet. People should never imagine that the game is exclusive to elderly ladies. It can turn into quite a battle. I have known people with the nicest dispositions become really ferocious at this underrated pastime. Then of course there is the sea within a short distance. If there is any sun about Kingsgate is certain to get its full share, and I have often been able to swim in the sea in November.

Mollie and I are both lucky in not showing our age too much. It is true that we both come from long-lived families, but I am sure that peace of mind is the real secret. I am indebted to Mollie for giving me that sense of tranquillity. She is absolutely perfect for me. I remember before we were married my mother said to Mollie, 'Whatever you do, don't try to tie him down.' Mollie has never attempted to, and perhaps that is why I have never tried to get away. The mutual respect and affection we share has been the foundation of our long and happy married life.

Many people brag about their independence and self-sufficiency and of not needing other people. I don't accept this attitude as credible. I think we all need each other.

I have written about my wife and the close friends who have done so much to make my work easier and my life happy. I would be less than fair if I failed to pay tribute to three other loyal folk who take care of our creature comforts so ably—Bob Court and Mrs. Mary Parfitt. Mary, whose husband John was a porter at the block of flats in which we lived in Regent's Park, has been taking care of our mews flat for some twenty-three years.

Bob is a true man of Kent or Kentish man—I am never really sure how it's applied. He lives today in the Ramsgate house in which he was born. His wife, Lillian, took care of the cottage until she died six years ago and Bob joined us there in August, 1950. We have to thank him for looking after the cars and the garden at Porsea when we are away, and also Mrs. Terry Salter who has worked for us at the cottage for the past seven years.

Then there are the past and present members of the *Dixon of Dock Green* team—like Geoffrey Adams, who played the part of D. C. Lauderdale, and my good friend Nick Donnelly, who still plays the part of Sgt. Wills— who have done so much to make the series a success for so long. When Ted Willis first suggested to the B.B.C. that *The Blue Lamp* could be adapted as a T.V. series a meeting was arranged between us and Ronnie Waldman, then head of B.B.C. Light Entertainment. Ronnie was very enthusiastic and asked me if I had any ideas about production if the project went ahead. I said I had. I was confident that the scripts would be available on time because Ted is extremely efficient and reliable, and I believed I had the answer regarding a director and producer. It was Douglas Moodie. He had brilliantly adapted *The Love Parade* film for radio in February, 1940, and it was logical that he must be my first choice to do a similar job with *Dixon.* This he did and successfully spearheaded production for seven years. His death two years ago was a great loss to T.V.

He was followed by directors who were no less distinguished —Barry Lupino (of the famous Stanley and Ida Lupino family), Ronnie Marsh, Vere Lorimer, Michael Goodwin and Robin Nash. More recently, there was a gentle break with tradition. A woman director, Mary Ridge, took over. I will admit that we had some misgivings when Mary's appointment was announced but these swiftly vanished when we saw how quietly efficient she was and the cast were very happy working with her.

She still works with our present director-producer, Joe Waters. He took over when I felt that the series needed a shot in the arm and administered the injection. Extremely varied scripts from an increased team of writers gave the series a new look.

All those friends I've mentioned in this chapter are now really members of Jack Warner's family!

Reflections

I SUPPOSE it is inevitable that having reached the age I have, and having spent so many years in show business, people should ask me questions on a variety of subjects.

Most people over fifty who see me still playing the part of George Dixon want to know what my recipe is for good health. I suppose I can sum it up in one word—moderation.

If they have any illusions about me having been a man who has fought off the demon drink or one of those stick-in-the-mud early to bed and early to rise characters they can forget such notions.

In between the wars when I was racing at Brooklands I was as happy as the next man—or gal—to stay on my feet at all night parties, but I had one golden rule, and that was to race first and celebrate afterwards. I've followed it too in show business—work first and fun later.

I used to enjoy a session on Scotch, but during my racing days I was putting on far too much weight so I cut out my whisky habit, and in two months I had lost a stone and a quarter. I remember one occasion in 1942 when I was a guest at the Officers' Mess after giving a show to the troops in

Huddersfield. I'll never know what brand of Scotch I drank that night and I'll never forget how ill I was afterwards. I didn't touch another drop of Scotch for about thirty years!

Sometimes I think that we can all become a little confused over what we should or shouldn't do about health if we watch every medical programme on television. Perhaps it's a case of regarding our bodies in the way I used to view motor cars. Certain engine adjustments and the use of different types of fuel will produce a better performance.

One of my friends in the motor business regularly consumed a bottle of whisky a day. He was as slim as a bean pole to the day he died—at a ripe old age. Another old chum in the business never took a drink before a show but consumed twelve bottles of Bass every night he came off stage.

My old boss, Maurice Sizaire, always drank wine and never spirits, and when he died at ninety-two he still had some hair and his own teeth.

At the time I had rejected Scotch while racing, I visited my doctor and told him I wanted to be at the peak of fitness for Brooklands. I was not a heavy smoker but he advised me to cut out cigarettes altogether. I went without a smoke for three months and really didn't get back to regular smoking for almost twelve years. Today, I'm happy with a pipe, enjoy cigars or have the occasional cigarette.

It is the osteo-arthritic condition I have in one leg which provides me with my only health hazard and as I mentioned earlier in my story, this resulted from the rough treatment my spine took in the film *Train of Events* and the jolting I received while racing at Brooklands. I think many people will agree that knocks like this which appear trivial when one is young can create problems in later life.

I consulted leading specialists about the condition of my leg and scrupulously followed advice and received treatment but it still gave me a great deal of pain.

Towards the end of a *Dixon* series in December, 1972, I became very worried about my condition and feared that it might even bring an end to my working days. It was particularly bad on what I call stop and start days when we have camera rehearsals and do scenes over and over again.

Having to remember words and actions, and also to worry about which foot I must put first to avoid stumbling, was not funny. I like to think that on these occasions I covered up very well—especially on one of my off days when I would have preferred certain critics to have been in my shoes and not sitting in comfortable armchairs writing snide comments about actors who should retire.

Before this particular series finished I began receiving letters from Mrs. Julia Owen, of Bromley, Kent, who said that she felt sure she could successfully treat me with bee venom.

By that time I had come to the conclusion that conventional medical practitioners could do no more for me.

On New Year's Eve, 1972, I was due to receive an award from the Variety Club of Great Britain. The presentation was to be made at *The Talk of the Town* at the London Hippodrome. As the award night drew near I became even more doubtful of my ability to climb the steps to the stage to receive the award from Mr. Bernard Delfont and decided to make an appointment with Mrs. Owen.

Mollie accompanied me and I was not a little surprised to learn that I was to be subjected to bee stings and that the treatment would take quite a long time. Two days before the New Year, Mrs. Owen put me in a herbal pack for eight hours each day, and by the second day the pain began to ease. I couldn't believe it! And I still had not yet experienced the bee stings!

On the all important evening we had drinks followed by a dinner and I suppose about three hours elapsed before I was called up on the stage. Normally, after being immobile for so long, I would have been forced to limber up, but when my name was announced I rose, mounted the steps and walked across the stage without any difficulty. I can truthfully state that it was the most exciting moment of my life—especially as the programme was being watched by millions who must have been well aware that I was limping a little towards the end of the *Dixon* series.

That incident was only the beginning. Two days later I had my first bee stings and, frankly, it was not as painful as I had anticipated. I had complete faith in Mrs. Owen because by that time I had learned something about her successes with patients over a period of forty years. Some people who have heard a little about Mrs. Owen's unorthodox methods appear to think that ordinary bees are used in the treatment but of course this is not so. They are specially bred and reared. After the first few sessions, I felt rather queer and experienced some strange dreams at night, but this was the result of the initial treatment. Certainly Mrs. Owen's achievements are astonishing. She has restored sight to people suffering from blindness (*retinitus pigmentosa*) and has effected cures in cases of asthma. Eventually, she hopes that the recognition her treatment has now received will enable her to establish a clinic in this country. As far as I'm concerned, I'm sure that but for her help, I may well have found it impossible to continue working and I am convinced that, with her continued assistance, I shall be able to carry on for as long as the public want to see me.

People often ask me when I'm going to retire and my short answer to that is never. I've always been extremely active and I hope to stay that way. A few years ago one of my uncles died aged ninety-two. He had always worked very hard and at the time of his retirement was an engineer at the local waterworks.

He and my aunt had bought a cottage in Ware, Hertfordshire, to live out their remaining years, and my aunt spent some time there every week preparing it for occupation. When the great moving day was accomplished, uncle and aunt went to bed early and were awakened the next morning by a fearful squeaking sound. My aunt explained to her husband that it came from a well. Water was hauled up each morning by the first villager to rise and the noise acted as an alarm clock for the rest of the inhabitants. This didn't suit uncle at all, so during the night he went up the hill to the well and oiled the gear. As a consequence everyone in the village slept on until 10 a.m. the next morning. Fortunately the identity of the phantom greaser was never discovered.

I thought the incident was gloriously reminiscent of a bygone age and in recalling it as I reclined in a garden chair on the lawn at our cottage I found my thoughts wandering to the show business days of the past and fairly logically, to the pattern of entertainment the British public might expect the profession to serve up in the future.

I think that we have been witnessing in the north of England clubs almost a re-birth of vaudeville as we knew it before 1914 and between the two wars. It is my opinion that as television gobbles up available material the standard of T.V. comedy will deteriorate. When this happens, the comedian appearing live on the stage will be contributing to a notable revival of the theatre we once knew. The beauty of vaudeville was that an artiste could tour with an act that was fresh to audiences in various parts of the country.

No less interesting to me is the obvious demand for more entertainment from the big bands as we knew them in the thirties and forties. I know that a mood of nostalgia exists everywhere at the present time and is exemplified by a growing interest in literature and films about the last war. Period plays and television series are enjoying unexampled success. I am convinced, too, that we are nearing the end of the pop group era. I watched the B.B.C. 2 series *Big Bands from the Dorchester* and I was gratified to see, when the camera panned to the audience, that at least half of the people present were between the ages of eighteen and thirty. This endorsed my belief that even the youngsters are now anxious to have the tuneless strummings of a few simple chords on a guitar replaced by something more melodious that they can whistle or hum.

Perhaps I'm kidding myself in thinking that most of the country's young people today would derive greater satisfaction from the entertainment that flourished between 1930 and 1950.

I am not suggesting that groups such as the Beatles didn't produce some pleasant melodies but many of the pop groups which followed would in my variety days have made the targets for cabbages, rotten apples and tomatoes.

Nobody will ever convince me that radio and T.V. networks are right to give air time to artistes bereft of talent, including those who have been dragged before the courts and convicted of drug offences. What must be the reaction of youngsters of good character? I don't think it's difficult to find the answer. When they see these degenerate teenagers screaming and shouting and trying to promote mass hysteria and read about their drug offences they must feel they, too, can make a pile of money by purveying entertainment that is rubbish and that drug-taking must be the 'in thing', otherwise their pop idols would not indulge.

Sometimes, as I mentioned earlier in this book, many parents write to me for advice about their problem children and it saddens me to learn of these family crises which stem from the participation of sons and daughters in the pop world and all the pitfalls inherent in that world.

I am well aware that hard commercialism is the basis of the pop industry. The output of tuneless records is the magnet that draws cash from the pockets of youngsters who have never before had so much to spend. I don't blame the kids who toss their cash across the shop counters in exchange for tripe. I feel sure that if the record manufacturers produced material of a higher standard youngsters would still buy their discs.

It will give me great personal happiness if I live long enough to see the nation's future parents growing up in a less violent society, and with a better sense of values in which they are concerned to help people rather than profit from them.

BIOGRAPHY

0352 Star

General

(all are illustrated)

	Doris Day & A. E. Hotchner	
395680	**DORIS DAY, HER OWN STORY**	95p*
	The Duchess of Bedford	
398078	**NICOLE NOBODY**	75p
	Max Bygraves	
396091	**I WANNA TELL YOU A STORY**	70p
	Diana Dors	
301589	**FOR ADULTS ONLY**	95p
	Peter Douglas	
300833	**CLINT EASTWOOD: MOVIN' ON**	75p
	Eric & Ernie	
300000	**THE AUTOBIOGRAPHY OF MORECAMBE AND WISE**	60p
	Margot Fonteyn	
397071	**MARGOT FONTEYN**	75p
	J. Paul Getty	
395362	**AS I SEE IT**	95p
	Noele Gordon	
300299	**MY LIFE AT CROSSROADS**	50p
	W. A. Harbinson	
301171	**EVITA (Large Format)**	£1.95
	Elizabeth Harrison	
301120	**LOVE, HONOUR AND DISMAY**	85p
	Frankie Howerd	
39594X	**ON THE WAY I LOST IT**	85p
	David Pryce-Jones	
30149X	**UNITY MITFORD**	95p
	Rene Jordan	
396873	**STREISAND**	75p
	Hildegarde Knef	
39644X	**THE VERDICT**	95p
	Lord Longford	
301473	**KENNEDY**	95p
	Lilli Palmer	
396083	**CHANGE LOBSTERS AND DANCE**	95p
	Jean Plaidy	
395044	**MARY QUEEN OF SCOTS**	95p
	Barry Sheene	
301430	**THE STORY SO FAR . . .**	85p
	Tennessee Williams	
395583	**MEMOIRS**	85p

† For sale in Britain and Ireland only
* Not for sale in Canada.
♦ Film & T.V. tie-ins.